HARD
Bastards 2

HARD Bastards 2

Kate Kray

**Pictures by
Geoff Langan**

JOHN BLAKE

Published by John Blake Publishing Ltd,
3 Bramber Court, 2 Bramber Road
London W14 9PB, England

First Published in Paperback in 2003

ISBN 1 904034 71 3

British Library Cataloguing-in-Publication Data:

A catalogue record for this book is available from the British Library.

Designed by GDAdesign

Printed in Great Britain by Bookmarque Ltd, Croydon, Surrey

1 3 5 7 9 10 8 6 4 2

NO WANNABES, NO PANTOMIME GANGSTERS, JUST THE HARDEST MEN IN BRITAIN

I DEDICATE THIS BOOK TO THE LOVE OF
MY LIFE, MY FRIEND AND CONFIDANT:
Leo O'Reilly

You may have noticed that there are only 24 men included in this book. There should be 25. Indeed, I interviewed 25, and 25 were photographed. But the 25th man was shot dead. A bullet through his head in a lonely country lane.

He was a dangerous man. He knew the risks he was taking and prison or death is the ultimate price you pay for living in this world.

I did not think it appropriate to replace him and unfair to his family to name him.

'Being in one of your books,
Kate, is like kissing the Queen Mum.
It's a great honour, but nobody
really wants to do it.'

'Gaffer'

Contents

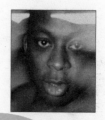

GARY HUNTER
79

STEVIE KNOCK
119

SID THE KNIFE
91

KEVIN CHAN
129

BAZ ALLEN
105

DANIEL REECE
139

stards 2

CHRIS MURPHY
149

JAMIE O'KEEFE
177

GEOFF THOMPSON
157

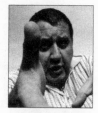

TREVOR
187

DAVE DAVIS
169

BRIAN THOROGOOD
195

HARD Ba

MARCO

DUCHY PETER

KALVINDER DHESI

DOMINIC

LOU YATES

MANCHESTER TONY

stards 2

GOVERNMENT HEALTH WARNING
THESE MEN CAN SERIOUSLY
DAMAGE YOUR HEALTH

ACKNOWLEDGEMENTS

A big thanks to all the men for telling me their stories. Also thank you to Roy Shaw, Joey Pyle, Vic Dark, Phil Grey, Stilks, Carlton, Linda Calvey, Sue & Vernon, Tony & Martin Bowers for making a few calls!

To Geoff Langan for the fantastic photographs.

To Mandy Bruce for all her hard work.

Geoff Langan would like to thank Pejeman Faraton at Fuji for his valuable contribution with this project.

FOREWORD

The men you are about to meet in these pages are hardcore. A hard core of hard bastards.

They're all extraordinary in their own way and they all have a tale or two. Some of the things they say are horrifying. They don't try to make excuses for their actions or justify what they've done. It's said and done, and that's it!

In the course of writing my books, I've interviewed hundreds of men and you quickly get to grips with who matters and who doesn't, who has respect and reputation and who hasn't.

Most of these men are aggressive in one way or another, many violent. Some will cut you and laugh while you're bleeding. All inhabit a world, a kind of parallel world, which ordinary people would find totally alien – they catch glimpses of it only occasionally on TV. But that's sugar coated. It's not the real thing. This is.

These men are an incredible bunch and, purely personally, it was an awesomee experience meeting and talking to them.

There's Carlton Leech, football hooligan, member of the notorious Inter-City Firm (ICF) and now minder, whose closest friend was blasted to death with a shotgun.

Charlie Seiga, from Liverpool, whom the police codenamed Killer.

Gangsters like Tony Lambrianou who stood with Ronnie, my husband, in the dock.

Danny Reece, an armed robber, who is married to Linda Calvey, the woman they call the Black Widow after the spider who kills her mate after sex. Both Danny and Linda are now serving life for murder.

Inside these pages, the best bouncers in the business, people like Stevie Knock reveal their secrets. And then there are the personal bodyguards and the pure fighters – champions in their own sphere, whether it be kung fu or bare-knuckle fighting.

There are heroes here – and, of course, villains.

After talking to so many of them, I can't help but notice how, despite the fact they are all so very different and such very sharp individuals, they have so much in common.

These are all hard men. Those on the right side of the law seem to have done OK for themselves and some – like Kevin Chan, the kung fu supremo, and Kiane Sabet, the hunky no-holds-barred fighter – are, I'm sure, destined for fame.

Those who have, shall we say, strayed across the line haven't always been so lucky.

Many of these men have had really difficult childhoods. Many learned to fight when they were young because they had to – from very early on the name of the game was survival. Many witnessed violence, either within their family or around them when they were youngsters. The education they received was poor and some of them didn't stand much of a chance. Most turned to crime to get money, pure and simple.

The question I'm asked continually – and usually it's more of an accusation than a question – is: 'Aren't you glamorising crime by writing about these people?

'Aren't you glamorising crime by writing about these men, by letting them tell their stories, by giving them airtime?'

The answer to that is: 'No, I'm not.'

No, no, no!

I don't write my books in a tongue-in-cheek way. I am fully aware that some of the things that some of these men have done is unacceptable.

Films like *Snatch* and *Lock, Stock* ... do much more to glamorise crime than I do. Those films are definitely tongue-in-cheek – they describe horrific crimes but put a joke or two in so that makes it OK. And everyone thinks it's OK. I tell it how it is, how it really is. I don't sugar-coat it. Because this isn't a glamorous world to be in. I think that often it's an extremely unpleasant world to be in. But people have always been fascinated by it, since the days of Robin Hood or Dick Turpin, and they always will be.

This is how it is.

So many of the men I have met have ended up spending the best part of their lives in prison – what a waste! As a result many of them have have lost their wives, their children, their homes. They end up with virtually nothing … and no one.

I can count on the fingers of one hand how many people in this world have come out with a fortune – most haven't got anything but diddly-squat.

People love to say that Ronnie and Reg earned bundles, and maybe they did, but most of what they earned they gave away – what could they spend it on?

I often think of Ronnie. I can see him sometimes when I close my eyes. I can see him and smile. Whatever anyone says we did have a genuine relationship and I can still see him now coming into the visitors hall in his fabulous suit, his crisp white shirt, gold cufflinks and Rolex saying, 'Hello, me Old Dutch, got any nooos?'

I made him laugh and I made him happy – as happy as you can be when you're banged up in Broadmoor for life. But was Ronnie ever really happy? And that's the point. Being banged up in Broadmoor – or any prison for that matter – isn't glamorous.

Was Reg happy? I don't know.

Was his life glamorous? No.

I don't glamorise crime. Ron and Reg were big time but, in the end, even if you are big time, one of three things are going to happen to you – either you will go to prison for a very, very long time, and like Ron you'll end up dying in prison; or, like Reg, they'll let you out just in time to die.

Or you'll end up being shot to death in a country lane.

I know many people in this parallel world and some of them are in their sixties, even their seventies, and they're still 'at it'. They still need the money. They're always looking for The Big One, the one that will set them up for life so they don't have to do it any more. That's the problem.

I like to call them the 'weekend millionaires'. You can always tell if they've been up to something because, come the weekend, they've got the Rolexes on, they've got the Armani suits on, they're being Charlie Big Bollocks in the pubs buying everyone a drink.

But if they can't keep up that lifestyle, then they have to go on to do another blag, or whatever it is they do. In fact, far from being glamorous, it's a very stressful world to live in. I think through writing these books and interviewing all these people, the thing that comes out of it most is that there's really nothing like a straight pound note.

So no, I don't think I'm glamorising them. Those who have stumbled on to the wrong side of the law, well, not one of them says it's a good world to be in because it's not.

But this is the truth. This isn't *Lock, Stock and Smoking Bollocks*. This is real. I tell it how it is. I tell it from the hip. And these men have been included in this book because *they're* going to tell you how it is.

HARD BASTARD

Carlton Leech

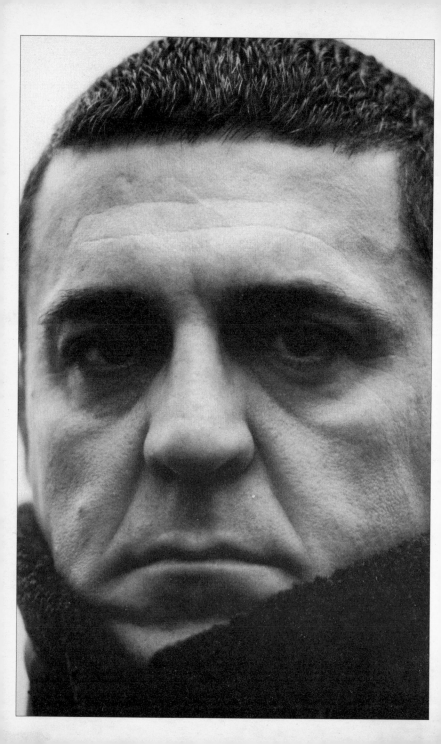

CARLTON LEECH

I'd heard of Carlton Leech – who hasn't? He has a reputation. A reputation as a hard bastard. A very hard bastard. And he had a history.

Who hadn't heard of the Range Rover murders? Three men found dead, blasted to eternity with a shotgun, in their Range Rover which was parked at the end of a lonely country lane in Essex. Some drug deal was supposed to be going down but it ended in blood, death and a lot of tears. One of the men, Tony Tucker, was Carlton's best friend. Carlton was his minder. For one reason or another, he hadn't been with him on that fateful night – if he had been, he would have got it too. Understandably Carlton was devastated by Tony's death.

The first time I met Carlton, I really didn't know what to expect. With a name like Carlton, I thought maybe he was black and I was quite surprised when he walked into

TFI Friday's on a wet Wednesday afternoon to find he was white. He's a good-looking man, despite all the knocks and bumps on his face, but there is a terrible sadness in his eyes.

In my opinion, what happened to Tony has been the biggest blow in his life. Carlton and Tony were mates, 'old muckers', and used to be together 24/7. That particular day, Carlton didn't go with him and I don't think Carlton has ever got over losing Tony. He has churned it over in his mind again and again, asking, 'Why? Why wasn't I with him when he needed me?' In a way, he blames himself and that's what you can see in his eyes.

Carlton carried Tony's coffin at the funeral and, when we were filming *Hard Bastards* for Channel Five, we took him to that lane and he became very emotional. By a strange coincidence, it was the anniversary of the killings.

He said he felt Tony all around him. At times, he stumbled over his words and he found it hard to go on. He did cry. Real tears and lots of them. Suddenly he said he didn't want to do the TV show – it was just too painful. But looking back at it now, he feels that going there helped him to release all that anger and pain. He said it was as if he was being exorcised.

After the initial shock of being in that lonely lane, Carlton recovered. He was apologetic, crazy and funny and quite easy-going. We must have looked a picture. He's so big we were like Little and Large.

One thing he couldn't do was bullshit me. When we were filming, he tried to tell me that he didn't take steroids.

'Not that old chestnut!' I said and laughed. Then he said he only took drugs to keep him awake.

'Yeah, and I'm the Queen Mother!' I said. And then we talked. He admitted he'd taken the lot, rooted and tooted big time – and steroids were the most terrifying. They'd turned him into a monster, a man who'd snap in a minute and use violence at the drop of a hat, a kind of Jekyll and Hyde person who could change from one to the other frighteningly fast.

The drugs had made him totally paranoid; he thought even his friends were against him, and he'd seriously thought about suicide. But Carlton is so strong he's got through it – at least, he's getting through it. These days, he keeps a low profile preferring to cook for his friends at home rather than going out. He has a girlfriend and life seems a little slower, calmer. But the paranoia hasn't left him – he's bought a flat which is on the third floor of a building at the end of a long cul-de-sac so he can see who's coming. That gives him time to get ready – just in case.

The past still haunts him and probably always will, but maybe that's what I found amazing about him. He's been through so much. He's lived life in the fast lane, he's been stabbed and shot at, he's been through the drugs nightmare, his best friend had his head blown off. At his lowest moment, Carlton just sat in the box room of his mum's house, with his hands in his head, in total despair, just wanting to die. But he's pulled himself through all that and he's getting on with his life, he's moving on. He's changed his life. He stared death in the face and spat in its eye. He said to me that he's a good boy now, a changed man, clean from drugs and crime. He told me, 'There's nothing like a straight pound note.'

Well, straight-ish ...

NAME: Carlton Leech
DATE OF BIRTH: 1 March 1959
STAR SIGN: Pisces
OCCUPATION: Enforcer

BACKGROUND

I was brought up in the East End, the Forest Gate/ Stratford area. My parents were out working much of the time so I had to take care of myself. There were lots of fights at school and outside. You had to learn to use your fists to earn respect and survive. I didn't like school but my dad was adamant that I should learn a trade. That way, he said, I'd always be able to find work. So, I started an apprenticeship in Engineering and Shipbuilding. As it turned out, Dad was right – after I left school I was never out of work. But outside school and work, football was my life. West Ham. The best.

I got involved with a gang which soon became known as the notorious ICF.

We'd meet up on Friday evenings in the pub and make arrangements for the following day's match. We planned it like we were going to war. And sometimes that's just what it felt like. It was a war of sorts. I have to admit that I loved the violence. The bloodier the better. It gave me that adrenalin buzz. Nothing like it. Eventually, it all changed.

Football hooliganism became a political thing. There were surveillance cameras everywhere and anyone who was suspected of causing trouble got banged up. Before, you'd just get a slapped wrist or a fine.

I started doorwork when I was 20. I worked some rough clubs and learned a lot. Then I moved on to bigger and bigger clubs until, eventually, I went into partnership with my friend Tony Tucker and we started a security firm. I was Head of Security at Ministry of Sound for a while, but we'd do security for anyone, anything. We were good. But there were a lot of drugs about and I took the lot – speed, Ecstasy, coke, steroids.

The steroids made me feel invicible. But they had a bad effect on me long-term. You think you can handle it easily, but your body can't. Tony and I became involved in dealing – we provided the muscle when deals were going down. And that was the end of it. Tony and two associates of mine were blasted with a shotgun in a Range Rover in a field in Essex. I should have been there, too, but I was on an attempted murder charge at the time and couldn't risk it. So I survived – even so, that was the end of it for me.

LIFE OF CRIME

I've been nicked, arrested for violence, grievous bodily harm and for possession of class A drugs with intent to supply but I've never been inside. Touch wood!

IS PRISON A DETERRENT?

Yes. I spent so much of my time when I was younger on visits to people who I cared for who were inside. Yes, it's a deterrent for me.

DO YOU BELIEVE IN CAPITAL PUNISHMENT?

Yes, for the right reasons. For anything where they've hurt children – I think they should be castrated or killed. Slowly.

WHAT WOULD HAVE DETERRED YOU FROM A LIFE OF CRIME?

I really don't know. Nothing really.

HAVE YOU EVER BEEN STABBED/SHOT?

I've been shot at, stabbed, glassed – oh, and I've had an axe in my head.

SCARIEST MOMENT?

I remember it well. I was on the door of a London club and I refused somebody entry. Later that evening, they came back with a gun. I couldn't – I wouldn't – run. I stood on the spot. I knew from the way he was holding the gun he wasn't joking, but I shouted at him, 'Fucking kill me!' He tried and the gun failed. That was a scary moment. Very.

SADDEST MOMENT?

My saddest day was when Tony Tucker was shot in the head. It was the saddest day of my life.

He was the other half of me. He was my brother. It's so true that when someone that close to you dies you feel like a part of yourself has died, it's gone, it's so painful.

WHAT RATTLES YOUR CAGE?
Imposters. I hate people who pretend to be what they're not. Plastic gangsters basically – they rattle my cage.

HAVE YOU EVER REALLY LOVED ANYONE?
My children. I really love them. And Tony Tucker. He was my friend and I idolised him as I was growing up.

WHAT FRIGHTENS YOU?
Me, myself, I.

DESCRIBE A HARD BASTARD
Someone who can stand there without weapons, without tools, and still win a fight. Someone like a boxer.

NAME A HARD BASTARD
Vic Dark.

WHERE DO YOU SEE YOURSELF IN FIVE YEARS?
Hopefully alive.

ANY REGRETS?
Sometimes I have trusted the wrong people. Funnily, I don't regret my past. I've done some wicked bad things but you can't reget your past. My past has made me the person I am today. I wish I could change some things ... but regret? Nah.

HARD BASTARD

Kiane
Sabert

KJANE SABERT

Kiane Sabet is the next Jean-Claude Van Damme just waiting to be discovered.

He walked into McDonald's to meet me wearing a bandana and a leather jacket, looking handsome, powerful and oozing confidence. Everything about him shouts confidence.

He's also a right hard bastard, one of the top bare-knuckle fighters here and in the States. That's no-holds-barred fighting, no rules, no preliminaries, just two men in a cage determined to beat the shit out of each other.

Kiane is extremely French – he's got the accent and the charm and, when he talks, he makes all the hand gestures. (Mind you, he eats for England – I mean, *three* McChicken sandwiches!)

Meeting him was quite an experience. He's so good-looking, he's got a great body (he showed me lots of photos of himself posing in the gym) and I wasn't surprised to find out that he's a real French charmer. Women just love him!

He seemed almost too handsome to be a bouncer. But he's worked all the top clubs and he admitted that he enjoyed all the girls he got to meet – gorgeous models, singers, strippers.

Kiane is bright, too – he speaks five languages – and he's ruthlessly ambitious. He's determined to make it and you can't help feeling that he will. Anyone that powerful and confident couldn't fail.

And there was one spooky thing. 'Where do you live?' I asked him.

'The East End,' he said.

'Whereabouts?'

'Vallance Road,' he said.

This man's travelled all over the world and now we meet up and he says he lives in Vallance Road. That's where Ron used to live. Un-fucking-believable!

NAME: Kiane Sabet

DATE OF BIRTH: 9 March 1973

STAR SIGN: Pisces

OCCUPATION: PBG (Personal Bodyguard)

BACKGROUND

I did my schooling in France then went to university for three years. Then we moved to Paris – I've got two brothers and a sister. I had everything I could have needed as a child and I love my family. My father had a good job. But I was always fighting as a child.

I started door work early. I did boxing at university and then started work as a bouncer in my spare time. Then I went into the Army. In France, everyone has to do national service, there's no choice. I found it OK but I wouldn't have liked to do it for ten years.

LIFE OF CRIME

I've never been to prison, although I've been arrested a lot of times. Always the same things – violence, fighting. But I wouldn't want to go to prison – I want my parents to be proud of me.

IS PRISON A DETERRENT?

It would be bad for my family to have someone in prison – and, for me, I would not like to be there.

DO YOU BELIEVE IN CAPITAL PUNISHMENT?

I think some people deserve it.

WHAT WOULD HAVE DETERRED YOU FROM A LIFE OF CRIME?

I've never been charged with anything – but then I've been very lucky.

HAVE YOU EVER BEEN STABBED/SHOT?

I have had a gun to my head but I've never been shot. Yes, I have been glassed in my face. I was attacked with a bottle and a knife but, no, I've never been shot.

SCARIEST MOMENT?

I'm not the kind of man who scares. I don't know what is going to happen in the future, apart from death, and I'm not going to think about that. Sometimes, when I'm involved in something, people say, 'Aren't you scared?' but I think the adrenalin takes over, you don't even think about it. You just do what you have to do.

SADDEST MOMENT?

I think I'm lucky because I'm not a sad man, I'm a happy man. The only time I can think of is when my grandad died. He was 98 years old so maybe that's not so sad. But it was sad for me.

WHAT RATTLES YOUR CAGE?

Disrespect. People with no respect rattle me. I respect people and I expect them to respect me; it doesn't matter what colour they are, I don't like people who are disrespectful.

HAVE YOU EVER REALLY LOVED ANYONE?

I'm not going to say how many women I have loved – that's not the question. I think I've found the love of my life. I want to be happy, be faithful to her, live together and have a family. We will have to wait and see, and only time will tell.

WHAT FRIGHTENS YOU?

Nothing much. But maybe the future frightens me ... if I get to 40 and I'm still a bouncer and I feel I haven't done anything with my life. Then I would not be happy.

DESCRIBE A HARD BASTARD

Somebody with no fear is a hard bastard, somebody who is a man.

NAME A HARD BASTARD

Any man who has the heart to stand up for what they believe.

WHERE DO YOU SEE YOURSELF IN FIVE YEARS?

If God is with me, hopefully in five years I will be doing something in TV or a movie, maybe a martial arts movie, but I won't do anything just to get there. If people want me, they've got to come to me, because if you're good, people will come to you, you don't have to go to them. I really hope to do movies.

ANY REGRETS?

Yes, I do regret I didn't do boxing seriously when I was 11 years old. Because I really believe that if I hadn't been so lazy as a child, I would be a world-class boxer by now. That's my only regret. Women haven't been my downfall – not any more. I don't get involved like that any more.

HARD BASTARD

Tony Lambrianou

TONY LAMBRIANOU

Tony Lambrianou deserves respect. He stood beside Ron in the dock at the Old Bailey in 1968 then he did 15 years for his part in disposing of Jack the Hat's body. He could have got a lesser sentence if he'd grassed on the twins, but he didn't. He kept his mouth shut, he did his time in some of Britain's toughest prisons and he did it like a man. For that alone, in my eyes he deserves respect – big time.

I first met Tony on the day I married Ron. He wasn't in Broadmoor with us for the actual ceremony, but he joined the gangster party we gave for 200 afterwards at a nearby hotel.

Tony looked – and still looks – just like you'd think a gangster should look, very Al Capone. He wouldn't look out of place in any of those old gangster movies. He was a good-looking man when he was younger. He's still a looker, but I think he has a sad face. He loves socialising and he's very much the perfect host, but perhaps what you see isn't what you get with Tony.

He has an amazing voice. The first thing that strikes you is this booming, deep, gravelly voice. If Tony says, 'Sit,' every dog in the room does – and not just the furry kind!

He's not a whinger but I don't think Tony has had an easy time of it. It must have been very difficult for him when he came out after 15 years with his name and reputation. He could hardly get a job serving behind the counter in the local post office, could he?

Instead, he's done the next best thing – he writes books, gives talks on the circuit about his past, his life, people he's known. A lot of people criticise him for doing that but, to me, he's got every right to do it. He lost 15 years of his life and where does a man like him go from there?

NAME: Tony Lambrianou

DATE OF BIRTH: 15 April 1947

STAR SIGN: Aries

OCCUPATION: Ex-gangster

BACKGROUND

I would rather not talk about my background. That is private, and I'd like to keep it that way.

LIFE OF CRIME
I've spent 15 years in prison.

IS PRISON A DETERRENT?
No. There's no benefit in it, nothing at the end of it. It just doesn't do any good.

DO YOU BELIEVE IN CAPITAL PUNISHMENT?
No, they've got it wrong too many times. The last ten people they hanged – they were all dodgy cases.

WHAT WOULD HAVE DETERRED YOU FROM A LIFE OF CRIME?
Nothing. Situation and circumstance made my life what it is.

HAVE YOU EVER BEEN STABBED/SHOT?
I've been shot at twice – a couple of people have taken pot shots. But I'm still here.

SCARIEST MOMENT?
Standing in the dock and being sentenced to 15 years. I was gutted. I looked at the future and I didn't like what I saw.

WHAT RATTLES YOUR CAGE?
False people, people who pretend to be something they're not.

HAVE YOU EVER REALLY LOVED ANYONE?
I think you can love anyone. I've loved other men as brothers, people like Ronnie and Reggie, Freddie

Foreman, friends. I loved my parents very much, my first wife and my kids – not forgetting my lady now, Wendy. I love her.

WHAT FRIGHTENS YOU?

I'm a bit long in the tooth to be frightened ... death, maybe. But we've all got to die sometime. So, nah ... I'm not frightened of anything.

DESCRIBE A HARD BASTARD

A man who stands by his principles, no matter what.

NAME A HARD BASTARD

Roy Shaw. A man would have to be brave or mad to take on Roy Shaw, the best bare-knuckle fighter in this country.

WHERE DO YOU SEE YOURSELF IN FIVE YEARS?

Hopefully just where I am now, enjoying my life. I'm happy where I am now.

ANY REGRETS?

You can't regret anything you've done; it's gone and that's that.

HARD BASTARD

Gaffer

GAFFER

'Fuck off! Fuck off! Fuck off!'

The manager in TGI Friday's was stunned and a look of fear crossed his face. Then Gaffer said, 'We're only going to be here for a short while, so fuck off!'

Needless to say, the manager fucked off. People tend to when Gaffer tells them how it is.

Normally in a man's company I wouldn't let people speak like that, but Gaffer is different. Gaffer is Gaffer. And the more I got to know him the more I understood that the manager's approach was making him feel embarrassed and uncomfortable so he wanted out of that situation as fast as possible.

Gaffer's been in prison a lot. He did 14 years last time and swears he was set up by some 'Northern shit' and that's made him bitter – especially about Northerners. He says he helped and trusted someone he shouldn't have.

Now he says, 'I never trust a Northerner.' He believes that Londoners who go to the North should respect their way of doing things – and very much vice versa.

'I said to these guys from Manchester, Kate, I said, "If I went to Manchester from London could I be the guv'nor?" They said, "No fucking way." So I said, "Well, it's the same here. If you're in London from the North, you should respect what Londoners are." '

Gaffer can talk the hind leg off a donkey and has an opinion on just about everything. He's done the lot. He's even been in politics. Believe it or not, he was a councillor and he got to meet Margaret Thatcher. God only knows what Maggie made of him. He is a wise-cracking gangster, if there is such an animal. But don't let his cheap gags fool you – he can be very menacing.

He's very alert when you meet him. He can sense trouble in the air before any other man. He says that when he's out, he likes to make sure he sits in a corner, he keeps his head down and he avoids unnecessary eye contact.

I visited his home and he has decorated his kitchen with crushed Coke cans and Kellogg's cornflake packets. In his garden, there are 'gravestones' engraved with the names of people he'd like to see gone … I think there's a lot of anger in Gaffer and he is ever so slightly off his fucking rocker.

'PS, Gaffer. Why are you called Gaffer?'

'My ex-father-in-law bought a business for me to run, a hairdresser's called Gaffer's. The name stuck.'

Oh.

NAME: John Pierre Rollinson – nickname Gaffer

DATE OF BIRTH: 5 April 1951

STAR SIGN: Aries

OCCUPATION: Professional lazy bastard!

BACKGROUND

I was born in Chelsea. My mother was Irish, my father was French. I was put in a home from the age of six months, a place called Tudor Lodge in Putney. And that's why I hate the Irish and the French because when I was born she fucked off back to Ireland and he fucked off back to France. I haven't got brothers and sisters as such, but because I lived with families like the Richardsons, and their family became my family.

I was in the home until I was seven, then I was fostered out to a family called Rollinson. I was always fighting as a kid. The reason the Rollinsons fostered me was because they had a son who was being bullied at school and my foster mum, Florence, wanted someone to look after him. My foster father was at the home and he saw me having a fight with five people because they were bullying someone and he said, 'I'll have him. If he can fight like that he can look after my son.'

LIFE OF CRIME

I've been to prison lots of times, I can't count how many times. I've only been in prison for violence, although my last one was for possession of drugs. I was disgusted with myself and that is the thing that turned my life around because I'm not a drug-dealer.

IS PRISON A DETERRENT?

No – it's a college. You get a petty crime-type person and he goes inside and he learns better things. So prison to me is a college. I've got a fucking degree!

DO YOU BELIEVE IN CAPITAL PUNISHMENT?

Yes – for paedophiles and for murder, by which I mean cases when people go around to other people's houses with the intent to murder. Not accidental murder. That don't count. Well, of course it does, but sometimes accidents happen.

The majority of crime doesn't deserve the death penalty but child abuse is different. For that, yes, capital punishment. Get rid of the vermin – why keep them banged up? It's just going to cost the tax-payer more money. Kill the scum in the worst, the most painful way possible. Make them suffer the way they made the poor children suffer.

WHAT WOULD HAVE DETERRED YOU FROM A LIFE OF CRIME?

I never thought I was living a life of crime. I was born fighting and being nicked is part and parcel.

HAVE YOU EVER BEEN STABBED/SHOT?

I've been stabbed four times and I've had a shot taken at me. Another time, someone went to shoot me and the gun jammed. When that fella was going to shoot me, for one second I did shit myself but when the gun didn't go off I looked at him and I said, 'Try again and see if it goes off.' But he didn't. So I winked at him and said, 'My turn.'

(Shortly before this book went to print, a professional hit was put out on Gaffer. Two men on motorbikes pulled up alongside him and tried to shoot him – they failed.)

SCARIEST MOMENT?

Being sent back to the children's home.

SADDEST MOMENT?

I've had a lot of sad moments, so I won't say the saddest. I've had too many sad moments. I'll tell you that when I give someone my loyalty, I give them my loyalty, and there's only one person who can break that and that's them. And when they do, that's a sad moment because they've now got an enemy.

WHAT RATTLES YOUR CAGE?

Disrespectful people, people who see you've got something and they want it but it's yours and they should respect that and leave well alone.

HAVE YOU EVER REALLY LOVED ANYONE?

My wife Wendy and my current girlfriend, Donna. I love her deeply, deeply.

WHAT FRIGHTENS YOU?

Losing Donna ... Apart from that, nothing. Although I get frightened sometimes when my girlfriend's out and I'm not with her. If anything happened to her, I know I would kill the man and then I'd go away. I know I'd kill them. That frightens me sometimes.

DESCRIBE A HARD BASTARD

I don't think I'm a hard bastard. But to me a hard bastard is a man who knows he's got the strength but he only uses force, violence, as a last resort, when he has to. In my mind, nobody is a hard bastard, they've always got a weak point.

People often say, 'Oh, so-and-so, he's a hard bastard,' but my first reaction is to say, 'How do you know? Do you know this for yourself first-hand?'

I remember when I was at the Ministry of Sound once and I pulled this geezer because of what he'd done to a friend of mine. Everyone said he was a hard bastard but he wasn't. I've got a megaphone in my car and I got the megaphone and shouted through it so everyone could hear, 'You're nothing but a worthless piece of shit! Come out, you wanker!' He was standing there by his car and did nothing.

I don't think of being a hard bastard, but when a job has got to be finished, it's got to be finished.

Let me explain. This man was shot three times and I met the man who shot him and he said to me, 'It was just a warning.'

No, he was wrong. I said to him, 'In my eyes, one up into the air and a gun to the head is a warning – right?

But you shoot a man three times and he's still alive in a year's time? That has now become an old score which has to be settled.'

In my eyes, if you shoot someone, you've got to shoot to kill because, if you don't, that person will be looking in the mirror every day, looking at their scar and they'll be thinking, This isn't right. They'll want revenge and, if you've done the shooting, there will be a time when you are vulnerable. There will be a time when you're off guard. But that person will be on guard, he's still got you in mind, he'll always have you in mind. You'll always have to watch your back, all day, all night, every day, every night.

NAME A HARD BASTARD
Dennis Richardson – known as one-hit Dennis.

HOW DO YOU SEE YOURSELF IN FIVE YEARS?
The one thing I've always maintained is that I won't die of natural causes.

ANY REGRETS?
No, I don't think so. The way I see it is: what will be will be. I have a lot of regrets but I can't change what's happened.

HARD BASTARD

Charlie
Seiga

CHARLIE SEIGA

Charlie Seiga's reputation is awesome, both in Liverpool where he comes from and around London. He was once one of the most dangerous men in Britain. Many men were murdered on Charlie's patch and many times the police marked him out as a killer. They even codenamed him Killer and, later, Charlie called his autobiography just that. The killings, I'd heard, were swift, brutal and brilliantly organised.

The victims had all been liberty-takers, vicious bullies, scumbags and no-marks. Charlie has been called a contract killer, a hit-man, a murderer. He's also been accused of being the brains behind bank raids, armed robberies and wage snatches which netted hundreds of thousands of pounds.

He's a straight-talking man with a code of conduct he lives his life by and, more importantly, he expects everyone else to live by it, too. He has no time for people who pick on the defenceless, the weak, the vulnerable, the elderly or women. In that, he's a villain of the old school.

I arranged to meet Charlie on a Thursday afternoon at my publisher's office in London. When I got there, Charlie was waiting for me, leaning back nonchalantly on a swivel chair. Being a gentleman he got up as soon as I walked in and greeted me by kissing my hand.

From that moment on, I didn't say much. Charlie talked, I listened. I watched him in that swivel chair, swinging non-stop from side to side, as he chatted and chatted in his Scouse accent, in a dialect that's completely alien to me.

When Charlie took a breath I tried to interrupt, but it was no use. Charlie was on a roll. He took a copy of my book *Hard Bastards* and started to give his opinion of the men in it. This one was a 'juiced-up doorman'; another was a 'waster'; that one was 'a soft lad'.

'They'd all be eaten alive in the 'Pool,' he said.

I started to get aggravated and twiddled my pen. I interrupted again – but I chose my moment carefully. 'Do you want to be in my book or not?'

He ummed and aahed. I could see him thinking, Shall I? Shan't I? He wasn't sure.

Five minutes, ten minutes. He chatted on. He told me about himself and there was no doubt that he was one hard bastard – he deserved to be in my book. But still he wasn't sure. Finally, I said, 'Well, are you going to be my Northern hard bastard or not?'

He smiled. Yes.

Later, I learned why he held back. Charlie doesn't want to be portrayed as a hard man because he says he's not a tough guy. I gave my word that I wouldn't distort the way I saw him and I won't … But …

He is a man who has done a lot of things in his life, always for a good reason – in his eyes. The way I see it, he's no angel. Then again, he's no devil either. We'll leave it at that. One thing for sure is that he is a gentleman. Recently, I had to go to Liverpool and Charlie and his friends met me. There was a limo waiting at the station and I have to say that I was treated like a princess.

Maybe it's called Liverpool hospitality. I'm not sure … Devil? Killer? But a gentleman, definitely.

NAME: Charlie Seiga
DATE OF BIRTH: 4 December 1940
STAR SIGN: Sagittarius
OCCUPATION: Restauranteur/chef

BACKGROUND

I was born in Huyton, Liverpool, and I wasn't born into a life of crime – far from it. Both my parents were as straight as they come. They were both honest, hard-working people. My mother ran a fish and chip shop.

We were a big family, I had six brothers and one sister, but my mother made sure we were always well dressed, unlike a lot of the other poor kids. Growing up as a child in Huyton in the Forties and early Fifties was great for me and my brothers. We were all comfortable and happy at home and we young ones wanted for nothing.

I became a villain from the age of 12. I think from an early age I wanted the good things in life, like fine clothes, cars and holidays. I had no intention whatsoever of earning my living honestly. I left school with no qualifications but I was offered the opportunity of learning a trade such as plumbing, bricklaying or joinery. But that wasn't the life for me.

LIFE OF CRIME

If I were to list everything I have ever done or been involved in or charged with, believe me, the list would be endless. I am no angel and I was obviously involved in a wide range of criminal activities for a long time. I have been charged with using and being in possession of firearms and other weapons such as hatchets, machetes and knives. I've been charged for GBH several times, as well as threats to kill, attempted murder and murder. I've been questioned many, many times. But the only convictions I have are three GBHs, the last of them being in 1966 – that's more than 35 years ago.

DO YOU THINK PRISON IS A DETERRENT?

It is and it isn't – it all depends on you. It's a matter of opinion that. Personally, I don't think so – you learn more about crime inside than out.

DO YOU BELIEVE IN CAPITAL PUNISHMENT?

Yes, I do for child molesting – not even killing a child, just touching a child – I'd kill them myself. Anybody who hurts children, in my eyes, just wants putting down. In fact, if I were in control of this country I might not even kill them – I'd just use them like animals are used for medical experiments. Instead of using the poor little animals, use these perverts, the real thing.

WHAT WOULD HAVE DETERRED YOU FROM A LIFE OF CRIME?

Perhaps if I'd been born rich, things might have been different ... I don't know. Things have changed so much. There's no respect left. There's no law and order. If you get into a row with someone over a little scratch on a car bumper, you're in real trouble.

But a woman gets raped around the corner or an old man gets mugged and the guilty get nothing, no punishment. Morals have gone. When I was a young man and I was a robber, I chose that path. My parents were good, clean-living, honest people but I didn't want to be clocking on at the factory and paying the mortgage for the rest of me life. I wanted more than that. There's no excuse for that.

In my day, you could walk in and out of a job. There was plenty of work for everyone. I chose my life, nobody corrupted me – it was all down to me.

HAVE YOU EVER BEEN STABBED/SHOT?

Yes, I've been stabbed, shot, mutilated, tortured, my lips torn off.

SCARIEST MOMENT?

Recently, I was tricked into going into this house in Liverpool. I got through the door of this house and I was attacked by a gang of drug-crazed scum, all off their heads on smack, crack and whatever else.

That was one of the scariest moments of my life because, let's face it, we're all scared of dying at times. We've all got to die sometime; it's just a question of when and where.

So I was ambushed by these guttersnipes – they're not interested in what or who you are – they're guttersnipes. They'll come out and pick on anyone – women, children, they don't care. I was sitting in the chair having been wrapped up and scalded and the skin was dropping off me. I was there for hours.

The next day, they realised who I was and this big black fella comes over and says, 'Listen, we respect you, Charlie man. But you're going to come back with us and we're goin' to whack you, we're going to do you.'

He pulled out a gun. And I'm tied up in this chair, ribs broken, stabbed, I'm done in, everything. I said, 'Listen ...' I was still trying to be a man, but I was shitting myself ... I was scared ... and I said, 'Don't do this. I've got a little daughter, she's got a right to a father ... don't do this ... don't do me in the face ... she'll have to identify the body ... shoot me in the heart.'

Then, just as he was about to pull the trigger, the little scum who tricked me in the first place jumped up and said, 'Don't kill him here, for fuck's sake, don't kill him here. His daughter has seen him getting in the car outside the house.'

Carlton Leech

Kiane Sabert

Tony Lambrianou

Gaffer

Charlie Seiga

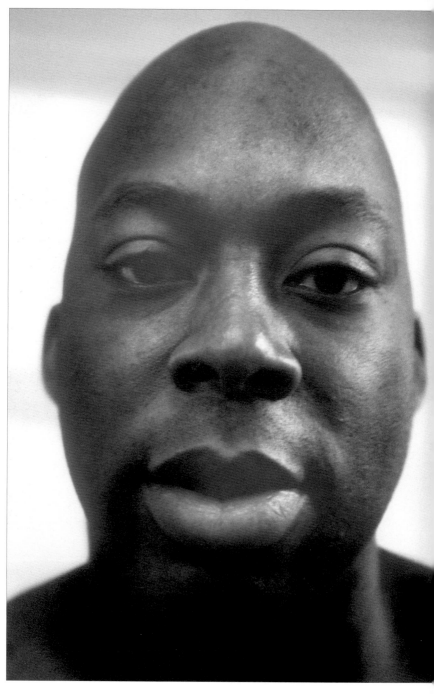

Ian Wadley

Gary Hunter

Sid the Knife

So I had a stay of execution. I was scared but then they were full of apologies, like they are when they've got off the drugs.

I'll never forget that.

SADDEST MOMENT?

That was when my sister died. At the time, I was charged with attempted murder and I was on the run. All the police in the north-west were looking for me, even the ports were blocked off down South. It was serious.

I'd stopped this man, he was an animal, a woman-beater. I was going to give myself up and I knew I was going to prison but my sister was dying of cancer. She was an angel, she was, never did anyone any harm in her life.

So I went to see her in hospital where she was dying of cancer and I knew I was giving myself up in an hour's time. And she's sitting up in the ward and all her friends were saying, 'Where's Charlie?'

Then I walked in with the flowers and she said, 'Oh God, Charlie.'

And I looked at her and I knew I wasn't going to see her again. When I turned away to leave she said, 'Charlie!' but I didn't turn around because the tears were welling up and I didn't want her to see me. I didn't want her to see me crying. I was trying to be a man.

WHAT RATTLES YOUR CAGE?

Lots of things. Liars. I *hate* liars. And what rattles my cage more than anything is lack of manners. We've all been brought up by good, decent people and we are decent people in our own way. OK, so I might have been a villain, a gangster whatever you like to call it – I'm not now – but people seem to take that as leave to be rude.

I hate people who underestimate your manners, your cleanness, all those things.

HAVE YOU EVER REALLY LOVED ANYONE?

Yes. On many occasions. I love women. My first great love was when I was 17. I met this smashing girl in the heart of Liverpool. But I was wanted by the police so we had to get out. We decided to go on holiday – but who goes on holiday in the winter? We didn't know where to go.

I was going around with £1,000 in my pocket and it's 1958. A lot of money. So we went over to the Isle of Man.

We loved one another, we'd plan the future and things like that. I'd known girls before but this was the real thing, it was magic. She died tragically soon afterwards and I was shattered.

WHAT FRIGHTENS YOU?

I wouldn't like to end up like John Gotti in a cage. I wouldn't want to go back to prison. I wouldn't want to go back for one day, one hour. That's my biggest fear. But I know that if I lost it, I could kill somebody – and I would if somebody touched my daughters or my family or my close friends. I'd go out and kill them and I'd think, Fuck the law, fuck the consequences. That's what I'm scared of.

DESCRIBE A HARD BASTARD

A hard bastard can be 5ft 3in, he doesn't have to be 6ft 6in. I know a man in Liverpool now who's 5ft 4in and he's got the strength of ten men. He's a lovely, lovely man, lovely manners, but he's striped people, stabbed people and to me he is the hardest bastard I've ever met. People always underestimate him; he's a businessman. I wouldn't call myself a hard bastard. I'm not such a hard-case.

NAME A HARD BASTARD

There's so many, it's impossible to name just one. These are men who don't go around looking to make a reputation, they don't boast, they don't have to.

WHERE DO YOU SEE YOURSELF IN FIVE YEARS?

On a yacht in the Med – surrounded by beautiful women!

ANY REGRETS?

No, it's my life, I wouldn't swap it for the world. I've sampled everything, I've been to the best countries, had the best jewellery, best cars. I've got three lovely daughters – one's a lawyer, one's a jeweller and one's in the medical profession. No regrets – I've had a fantastic time.

I've written my own epilogue and this is it:

'Throughout my criminal career, I was very loyal to my own kind or, should I say, anyone who was involved with me in any criminal activity. I always made sure when planning and executing any sort of robbery, or any other crime, my friends and family who were involved with me could rest assured that their liberty would never be jeopardised. If the work we were carrying out did not look right, even if a blade of grass was out of place, I would insist we pull out. After all, my top priority was to stay free and thieve another day.

'I am fully aware that certain people have branded me a "killer". I would like to state I am not a psychopath. I would not get a thrill out of killing someone just for the sake of it. I am not a callous or cold-blooded person. I love my family and true friends to whom I would give my undying loyalty. I believe nearly every one of us, especially men, have the killer instinct in us. How many people can honestly say they have never thought about having, or would like to have, somebody killed? To kill someone is easy. The hardest part is the planning and organisation and getting away with it.

'My only regret is there are four or five people who are scum-dog enemies of mine and still living who shouldn't be, in my eyes. I would have no compassion or hesitation to have them killed but, like I say, it's the getting away with it afterwards.

'Revenge is sweet. As long as I get revenge, no matter how long it takes, to me it is the most satisfying sensation there is. Certain people have given me secondary information, of course, that I am going to be shot or killed. All I can say to that, to whoever they are, is – make sure you plan it properly and make sure you've got the bottle to put one in my head instead of half-heartedly in my leg. If you are going to do the job, do it properly. After all, we have all got to die sometime. It's just a matter of when and where. Maybe one day my luck will run out. Well, if that is the case, so be it.'

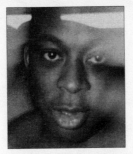

HARD BASTARD

Jan Wadley

IAN WADLEY

Ian Wadley is a big, powerful black man. You'd never knock this man over – he's solid all over, as wide as he's tall. When he was doing five years for armed robbery, he met a screw called Gary Taylor who recognised his natural strength and encouraged him in body-building and weight-lifting. Since then he's been in championship contests for both – he's lifted 600 kilos! – and it shows. Ian is fit, although not as fit as he was. In November 2000, he was shot in the back and leg when someone tried to murder him. He's also been axed in the leg and stabbed three times.

When I first met him, I didn't think he looked like an Ian. His looks and size and power just don't suit the name. I thought he should be called something else – Razor, for example! He didn't agree with me.

Instead, I nicknamed him Prada because of the way he looks, the smart way he dresses; his image is so important to him. He's got to have the best of everything. He's got over £40,000 worth of clothes in his wardrobe, all the best designer gear – suits, shoes, the lot. I can't imagine Ian would ever wear anything from Marks and Spencer and when he goes out he really does look the biz! So, I call him Prada.

Ian is a hard bastard, no doubt about it – he's been picked up for three murders, not to mention the armed robberies. But behind the toughness there's real gentleness. He's so quiet and polite, almost humble. In my experience, they are the most dangerous.

And he's obviously madly in love with Sarah, a gorgeous Page 3 girl and lap-dancer – he can't watch her when she dances at the club. He waits upstairs while she's doing her turn. (I watched and she was amazing – like Olga Korbut on acid!)

Ian couldn't have been more helpful when he appeared in my first TV series of *Hard Bastards*. He let me into all parts of his life. He let me see his world, his house, his business, his gym and he's an extraordinary man, the kind who sets himself a goal and goes all out to achieve it. Then, having done that, he drops it and goes on to the next goal. Always higher, always better, always more.

He let me into his world, but I couldn't help feeling that Ian is a very secretive man; he plays his cards close to his chest. I know he is a dangerous man but I didn't see him as intimidating. And yet ... and yet ... I felt there were deep, dark secrets that I hadn't yet uncovered. I couldn't – or Ian wouldn't let me – uncover.

NAME: Ian Wadley
DATE OF BIRTH: 24 March 1966
STAR SIGN: Aries
OCCUPATION: Fixer

BACKGROUND

I've got brothers and sisters but I was lonely as a boy. I don't want to say why I was unhappy, I just was. It upsets me to think about it, let alone talk about it.

LIFE OF CRIME

I've been in prison for an armed robbery. My job was to go in there and get the safe out – that was my main job. I got five years for that. I've been arrested three times for murder, once for armed robbery. Shootings, stabbings, things like that, mainly being in the wrong place at the wrong time. Honest!

IS PRISON A DETERRENT?

No. But I wouldn't want to go back inside. Having said that, I'm old-fashioned. If it was a friend, or someone I'd known for a long time, and they were in trouble, I would go out of my way to do something to help them, whatever that meant. I would probably regret my actions because it would be a long time inside or whatever ... I'd stop and think ... but I'd probably stop and think after the crime.

DO YOU BELIEVE IN CAPITAL PUNISHMENT?

No. Well, yes and no. It depends on the crime. My answer would probably be yes if it was a child molester or something like that, or someone who was going around raping kids. If it were a daughter of mine, I'd kill him myself. But anything else ... it's a difficult question, isn't it? ... Getting rid of someone full-stop.

WHAT WOULD HAVE DETERRED YOU FROM A LIFE OF CRIME?

A better upbringing, I suppose. It's the way I was brought up. I come from a working background. My dad was a builder and plumber – now, in some families they'll push their sons and daughters in the right direction. But in our family, my dad was all 'Do this' and 'Do that' and a few years ago my old man said, 'No one's taking my place,' or whatever and my brother said, 'Well, push us in the right direction.' He could have done but it wasn't like that in our family. And that's why I took to crime and things like that.

But I suppose I'm too old to make excuses now. It's not just about money – if I'd been pushed in the right direction, I would have got a better education, a better job. As it was, I ended up doing silly jobs like being a 'gofer' – all sorts. I worked for Barclays Bank for a few weeks, as it happens!

HAVE YOU EVER BEEN STABBED/SHOT?

I've been stabbed in the arm, stabbed in the tops of my legs, I've been shot in the legs and I've still got a bullet in the kneecap. I've been shot in the back and macheted in the leg. Yes, I've been through it all.

SCARIEST MOMENT?

I should say being shot is my scariest moment. Being shot is pretty scary.

SADDEST MOMENT?

I'd rather not say.

WHAT RATTLES YOUR CAGE?

Not much. Except bullies. Bullies rattle my cage. They have ever since I was bullied as a boy.

HAVE YOU EVER REALLY LOVED ANYONE?

Sarah, my girlfriend, my partner. I've been straight with her. I've told her everything. She knows everything about me. I know everything about her. We have a really good relationship because it's based on trust.

WHAT FRIGHTENS YOU?

Sarah and rats! I do like to go out with my mates but people will always rat on me to Sarah! Nine times out of ten, if I go to a club there's a friend of Sarah's working there! Perhaps I spend too long speaking to one girl – and they rat on me! That's frightening!

DESCRIBE A HARD BASTARD

Most hard bastards are quiet but there's something about them; it's the way they walk, their presence, their aura, people around you know if you've got it, they can feel it.

NAME A HARD BASTARD

Johnny Adair. I know some Irish people who know him and if you do something to him he'll come back to you the next day. He's a fearsome, fearless man. Do something to him and he'll come after you and I do respect him.

WHERE DO YOU SEE YOURSELF IN FIVE YEARS?

Owning a couple of villas, hopefully settling down, getting married. Having a good family life, really – that's the most important thing.

ANY REGRETS?

No regrets at all. No. Being in prison taught me how to survive on the street. If I never achieve anything, then I'll have regrets, but so far I have no regrets. I've achieved things. I've travelled all over the world. I've done my fair share of things on my own so I haven't got any regrets.

I wouldn't mind going into films but nothing major – a small part or something would be good – I'd like to be an actor, but nothing major – an *EastEnders* role maybe! Or perhaps I could work for Guy Ritchie or someone like that!

HARD BASTARD

Gary
Hunter

TOMMY

HILFIGER

GARY HUNTER

Meeting Gary Hunter – ex-soldier and now minder to the rich and famous – was an odd experience.

I sipped my café latte in the lounge of a posh hotel waiting for Gary to arrive. I glanced at my watch. Bang on 7.00pm – the appointed time – the automatic doors opened and there he stood. Not what I expected, not at all. He was small and wiry with penetrating blue eyes.

From the moment he sat down, he didn't stop talking. Usually, I'm the one who does most of the talking! But not this time. Gary wasn't the run-of-the-mill hard bastard I'm used to interviewing. He was different. Of course, we've all got our own opinions about politics and the like but his ideas *consumed* him; he was anti-Government, anti-establishment, anti just about everything.

He was very well versed in army matters. He knew all about 'covert operations', 'intelligence surveillance', gadgets and guns. He spoke at length about things I'd never given any thought to and he gave me answers to questions I'd never even asked. Yes, he was different; thought-provoking, intensely passionate about his beliefs, banging the table with his fists to emphasise a point – and spilling my café latte in the process, then mopping it up without drawing breath.

As we left the hotel, I asked him where his car was parked. He pointed to a dimly-lit side road beyond the hotel forecourt.

'I was here an hour before you,' he whispered. 'I sussed the joint out and watched you arrive.'

He shook his head at me and smiled a strange smile: 'Well,' he said, 'better the hunter than the hunted …'

NAME: Gary Hunter

DATE OF BIRTH: 30 September 1963

STAR SIGN: Libra

OCCUPATION: Bodyguard

BACKGROUND

I was brought up in a little fishing village on the east side of Scotland, but I suppose my accent has changed because no one down here in the South knows I'm a Scot. Even so my accent comes right back when I talk to my father!

The village was divided into four areas with invisible

boundaries, and groups from each used to fight each other. I ended up fighting the lot!

I was an only child and I trained in the martial arts from the age of nine. I did Thai boxing for eight years. I've fought in France, Belgium, Denmark and Holland.

I got married last year and I've got one child, a beautiful little girl.

LIFE OF CRIME

Nothing much I've ever been caught for. I've been arrested on several occasions for violence. My prison record reads nothing else – violence.

IS PRISON A DETERRENT?

No. I've only done time on remand so obviously I can't speak for long-term prisoners. But, from what I've seen inside, all they try to do is destroy your train of thought. They do your thinking for you. They give you breakfast at half-eight, dinner at twelve, tea at five – it's up to you to keep your mind working while you're inside.

Prison didn't deter me from anything – it's other people in the business who have deterred me. I think in this day and age there's so few people you can trust – people you can trust just aren't out there any more. I've seen some people fuck over their best mate for a pound note and that's not the way I was brought up, that never happened then. Money has become more important than friendship. People's loyalties seem to be determined by one thing only – and that's money.

DO YOU BELIEVE IN CAPITAL PUNISHMENT?

Yes. I was brought up with the belt. I believe in an eye for an eye, a tooth for a tooth. I don't believe in hanging for murder – I think they should be put through what their victims were put through.

It's crazy. Someone bursts into your house so you bash them up – but you're not supposed to do that no more, are you? You're supposed to pick up the phone and say, 'Look, there's someone in my house. Can you come round here and get them out?'

Well, that isn't a natural human instinct if someone is threatening your family and children. It's like with an animal – if you try and take its young, it will go for you. We think we're so much better as human beings, but we're not.

I don't believe capital punishment should be by lethal injection – that's just putting them to sleep. That's what we do to pets in pain – pets that we love. Why should you give that to someone who's done something really bad? I believe in the very, very old ways.

WHAT WOULD HAVE DETERRED YOU FROM A LIFE OF CRIME?

I don't think I've had a life of crime. We've all done things illegally obviously. What is crime? It's what the Government tells you is crime. They say you can't do that, so it's a crime. Just because they say it isn't right to do it, doesn't mean that, in my eyes, it's not right to do it. What they say is a crime I don't necessarily see as a crime. I earn my living my way because they won't let me earn it any other way.

HAVE YOU EVER BEEN STABBED/SHOT?

I've been stabbed and I've been shot. I have a hole in the bottom of my back and in my nipple and at the back of my head.

SCARIEST MOMENT?

It was in a club in Colchester and big group of doormen had come up there for a stag night. This one big geezer was threatening a little geezer – he was bullying him and there's no need to bully anyone, there's no reason to invade anyone else's space. So I said, 'Come on, mate, leave it. 'He's only half your size so there's no need to pick on him. Go and pick on someone your own size.

He was a fucking big bastard and he said he couldn't give a shit.

He walked off but then I saw him in the corner with six others, all big lads, and I was on my own. So I went behind the bar. Suddenly they came rushing at me behind the bar, they knocked the doorman out and I was alone with 11 of them. I escaped to the kitchen but they followed me. I got in a few punches but they were hitting me with everything – fire extinguishers, soup ladles, you name it. That's where I got all the cuts on the back of my head but I never actually went down.

Then one of them tried to rob my pockets and that did it.

I managed to kick one and punch another and that gave me a bit of space so I could run off down the corridors, slamming all the doors behind me. I had blood coming out everywhere.

Then I got into the toilets and there was a skylight with wired glass in it – and that was the only way out. There was a bang on the door. I opened the door and hit him. He went down. His mate was outside in the corridor running up and down – it was only a matter of time.

I managed to punch my way through the skylight, I cut my hand to fuck but at least I got out on the roof. From there I could see them come out the back and one of them said, 'Oh fuck it, the little bastard's scared, he's fucked off.'

Well, that was enough for me. I jumped off the roof into the lot of them. I nutted one, hit another, then jumped over the fence into a garden and off. They followed and there were two of them faster than the others – it's always the way, Kate. There's always two who are faster than the rest. So I stopped and hit both of them.

I got away. But, I tell you, when I was actually trapped in that kitchen, I was scared. That was one of the scariest moments of my life because I was getting it from all angles.

SADDEST MOMENT?

My mum died of cancer when I was 21.

WHAT RATTLES YOUR CAGE?

Bullies. You see these so-called hard men and they're not hard men, they're bullies. There's no such thing as a hard man. Every man's got a chin. All you've got to do is find his before he finds yours. It's up to you to prepare yourself to do that. There's no such thing as a lucky punch – well, maybe sometimes, but very rarely. It's up to you to know what you're capable of and to do it. But if you go into a fight thinking you're better than the next man you'll lose anyway.

HAVE YOU EVER REALLY LOVED ANYONE?

Yes, big time. I love my wife, Jo. Our relationship was on and off for a few years but I'm married to her now.

I suppose the person I have loved most was me mum, maybe because I didn't have brothers and sisters. I was really close to her. I was outraged when she died of breast cancer. She never smoked, never drank, never did a bad thing in her life. She had both breasts removed, then all her hair went. I was helpless but I felt outraged to witness what that did to her as a woman. I was a nasty person then. I was the nastiest person I knew then, I was the kind of person I'd hate now. I couldn't understand why it was happening, I didn't give a fuck about anything or anyone.

DESCRIBE A HARD BASTARD

I'm ex-military and I'd describe a hard bastard as someone who can cope with all sorts – extremes of temperature, hot and cold, near-starvation, being able to go on when you can't go on no more. When it comes to a fight, how many fights last longer than a few minutues? Very few. I admire boxers. You look at a professional boxer, how long is he fighting for? He's got to dig deep like he's never dug before. Each round is three minutes. People think that's nothing but it's a lot. You get the average man off the street and tell him to punch a bag, shadow box, for three minutes and he won't be able to do it.

A hard man to me is definitely a man who doesn't use a tool. Don't get me wrong, there's times when you have got to use tools, but a hard man, if there's a row, he'll fight you toe to toe – he won't pull out a knife and kill you. A hard man can stand there and he'll take a punch but he'll get over that and he'll return it back.

NAME A HARD BASTAARD
Rocky Marciano.

WHERE DO YOU SEE YOURSELF IN FIVE YEARS?
If only we knew where we'd be in five years! Well, there's only one person it depends on – it's up to me. There's so many people wandering around with no direction. It's up to you to make your future. I've got a direction.

When I first came out of the services, I found civilian life fucking boring; there was nothing to do. I was in for six years and what I've done is turn around all that knowledge and use it. I still keep up the fitness, I train all the time. Of course, in the services, you're told what to do, you get your orders for the day, but you don't mind doing it because you know that the people who are telling you have been through it themselves.

I know what I did in the marines and I know I'm good at what I do. I've used that. Now I do bodyguarding, I m working to get my certificate with the SAS up in Hereford because it's the only one that's recognised within the industry. It's not like the normal nine-to-five job and yes, there's aggression involved, but that's all I've ever done. I went straight from school into the forces, then I did my marine course then I became a PT instructor and then my mum developed cancer and that's why I left. If that hadn't happened, I'd still be in there because I loved it. I travelled the world, I've been all over the world – Far East, everywhere.

I've always had a sense of adventure. Maybe it's to do with being an only child. If you've got brothers and sisters you've always got someone to play with; if you're an only child you've got to find someone to go and play with, which I think makes you an outgoing person anyway. I have a direction and I'm happy with that direction.

ANY REGRETS?

Yes, I regret giving my friendship to some people who I now know didn't deserve it. I gave my loyalty, I'd have given my life for these people and I thought they would have done the same for me.

I can't say if I've done things I regret, I suppose the answer to that must be yes and no. I rarely do things I regret because I think things through carefully before I do them. That's training I suppose. I don't really act on impulse and I don't have time for regrets. It's all down to yourself.

For example, you can't get grassed up. If you get grassed up it means that you've told them or you've told someone who's told them. It's up to you. The only person responsible for your life is yourself. If you give your word to a best mate, then you've got to think, 'Can I trust them?' There's not that many people out there you can give your word to.

If you only give that word to yourself, then you've only got yourself to worry about and if you work alone, you won't get caught because nobody knows – the only person who can get you caught is you – nobody else can. People say, 'You grassed me up' – I'll say, 'You grassed yourself up, you stupid mug.'

It's like a chain. The shorter and fatter a chain, the stronger it is – the longer it is, the thinner it is, the weaker it is. That's why you keep things to yourself. The more you tell other people, the weaker that chain is. And that's how I've always lived. And that's why I haven't done any bird.

HARD BASTARD

Sid the Knife

SJD THE KNJFE

Sid the Knife ... just the name conjures up all kinds of things you'd rather not think about.

We went to meet him at a service station on the M25 on a wet, horrible, rainy Tuesday night and were just having a cup of coffee when in walked two policemen, then another two, and they sat at a table behind us.

This wouldn't do. There was no way that Sid would talk with four Old Bill sitting immediately behind him; he'd feel decidedly uncomfortable. Then in came another two and joined the others and now there were six.

I moved tables – and just in time, for in walked Sid – a 6ft-something black man with long dreadlocks and, I have to admit, a shifty look on his face.

He said quietly he'd left his tools in the car – he felt naked without them. It was the first time he'd gone in

anywhere without a tool for years. I was slightly uneasy –
all I knew about him was his name.

But he turned out to be not what I expected at all. He
was so polite, so respectful, a pleasure to talk to. What
impressed me was that he seemed so aware of how people
could look at him and get the wrong idea – i.e. feel a bit
scared. He said that when he walked down the road, he
always crossed to the other side if there was a woman
walking ahead – he didn't want to alarm her.

He honestly respects women and he talked a lot about
his mother. He said it was a privilege to talk to me –
which was nice – and he talked about the respect he had
for Ron because he had set standards for the underworld
which were based on respect. Sid is a very moral man, a
deep thinker – and, as he liked to put it, without morals
'it's a dog-eat-dog world'.

He didn't like criticising people without knowing them
– he likes to make his own mind up about people. He
doesn't like gossip or hearsay. If someone says someone is
a wrong 'un, he'll decide for himself whether it's true. He
won't be told – make a friend of Sid and you've got a
friend for life.

He had a lovely sense of humour. He said, 'I suppose
you want to photograph me with a big knife!'

'Yes, please,' I grinned.

In fact, I was surprised he agreed to be in this book at
all, but he laughed and said, 'You're nobody unless you're
in somebody's book these days!'

Oh.

The more we talked, the more I puzzled about his

nickname – Sid the Knife. He just didn't look or sound like a mad knifeman to me.

'I used to like a bit of Charlie in the past,' he confessed. 'I used to snort it off a knife, a small knife, so I'd carry that knife with me. Then, as the lines got bigger, so did the knives! That's how it started, so I'm Sid the Knife ...'

Well, that's a relief ... I think!

NAME: Sid – just call me Sid – that will do
DATE OF BIRTH: 21 March 1964
STAR SIGN: Aries
OCCUPATION: Transport driver, ex-doorman

BACKGROUND

I was born in south-east London then moved to the East End when I was about seven. I've got four brothers and two sisters. One brother and a sister are in the Caribbean, the others are here. My parents went back to the Caribbean for a while when I was growing up and then I lived with a white foster family and their kids became my brothers as well. Because we were split up at times, I met my real brothers and sisters at different ages. I met one sister when I was 11, met another brother when I was 13 and another when I was 15.

I had a normal kind of upbringing; you know, going to

school, doing sports, athletics and things. I always wanted to be a body-builder – even though I was 6ft 4in I wanted to be big! I remember seeing a geezer walking down the road when I was about 15 and as he was getting closer to me he was getting bigger and bigger. He had this little bag in his hand and I looked at him, at this huge geezer, and I thought, I want to look like that. So from the age of 15 I started training. As a child, I knew hardship; we didn't have holidays, no new shoes, that kind of thing, but it was a good life and I never begrudged my mum for not giving things to me because I could see, watching her struggle, that that's how life goes sometimes.

I used to have fights at school but I was respected as well. There weren't many black kids at school and you get problems in the third, fourth and fifth years. I suppose race and colour had something to do with it, but because I went to school with my white foster brothers we all dealt with it ourselves. I always tried to be friends with everyone. I was always friends with the girls!

At home, I've never believed in all that effing and blinding in front of your parents. If I had done that, my mum would have given me a clip round the ear! She'd still give me a clip round the earhole now! When you go in your mum and dad's house you've got to behave; when you walk in that door you've got to behave like a son. Whatever you do, you don't bring it home.

I left school young. My first job was working on a building site and I used to give my mum my wages every week. I always looked after my mum, that was my first priority. As a teenager, I was never one for going to football matches. From the age of 14, I was going to clubs locally and up the West End. I started working the door at 17.

One day, when I was training, I met Carlton Leech and we got talking. He said, 'Come on, I'll look after you, son.' He taught me bits and pieces and I got introduced to loads of people. We're like family now – he's helped me through thick and thin. He's been there when things haven't worked out for me. He's met my mum and dad. They took him in and called him 'son' so, as far as I'm concerned, he's my brother. If my parents have given him that kind of recognition, that's good enough for me.

If there's anything I want to do – like this interview with you – I ask his permission. If there's anything I've got to do, like debt-collecting or personal minding or working the door, I talk to him first. Don't get me wrong, I've got my own views and he asks my opinion for certain things, too. But I feel it's a duty; if you're that close to someone, you can't simply go out doing your own thing ... respect. That's what it's all about. If you've not got that, then you have nothing.

LIFE OF CRIME

I've been arrested by the police but I've never been in court, never been nicked. I try to be as straight as possible because I've got no time to mess people about. I look at it this way: if you're in trouble and you need help, I won't turn my back on you, I'll help you out if I think it's right even if someone else says, 'Don't, they're no good.' If you ask me for help my loyalty goes right down to the end.

People can say I'll die for you and all that, people can talk it and people can do it. I do it.

IS PRISON A DETERRENT?

It's a deterrent for the everyday, nine-to-five working person. It does deter those people. But, for people like us, it's like in the back of our minds. Whatever we do, we try and keep one step ahead of the Old Bill. That's the name of the game in our own community.

For a lot of people, prison is no deterrent at all, people like rapists and paedophiles. Prison doesn't deter them because they seem to be lost in their own world. I can't tolerate men who abuse women and children. I can't stand the fact that there are people out there doing things to these children. If a child molester lived round the corner, I'd knock at his house and I'd knock him out. Because, at the end of the day, *that* kid is *my* kid, even if I haven't got kids.

DO YOU BELIEVE IN CAPITAL PUNISHMENT?

Yeah. People say taking the law into your own hands is wrong, but what if it were a member of your own family? You'd want revenge. Then there are people like rapists, stalkers, people who hurt children. You have to have a line somewhere.

WHAT WOULD HAVE DETERRED YOU FROM A LIFE OF CRIME?

I've never had a life of crime as such. Crime has been around me and I've witnessed certain situations. But what is crime? It's easier to do something bad than to do something good. I mean, if there was a tenner on the floor, would you pick it up and hand it in? But how many people do that? It's easier to put it in your pocket. People say, 'I found it so it's mine,' but it ain't yours.

But to do something good like hand it in to the police station isn't easy and, if you do, people say you're mad! So what could have deterred me from doing that?

My life is what it is. It's got nothing to do with my family upbringing. Maybe if I'd had the opportunity to educate myself a lot more it would have been different, if I'd had the education to get a proper job, to establish myself on the ladder and go up in society. Maybe then I wouldn't be here now. I'd be out there earning loads of dough, living in a nice house, enjoying nice this, nice that and the other.

But these days, everyone seems to be going down the ladder towards crime. Everyone is thinking, I can earn a monkey tomorrow if I do that and who's going to know?

HAVE YOU EVER BEEN STABBED/SHOT?

Er ... yes, come to think of it, I have been stabbed, many, many years ago. Does that count? I've been shot at as well.

SCARIEST MOMENT?

Scary moments are when you're trapped in a corner and you know there's only one way out. Or getting the phone call which says, 'You've got to go now.' That's the scariest moment. No matter how people say, 'Yeah, I'm up for it, I'm up for it,' it's scary.

You're sitting indoors, watching the telly and all of a sudden you get the phone call and someone says that whoever has been shot. Whatever you're doing, you think, Right, what have we got to do? All your emotions are suddenly tight. You might be feeling confident with ten people around you but this only involves you, you as an individual and that's what's scary.

The scariest person is yourself because when you look in that mirror, there's only one person you see. When you open that door, who goes through that door? Only you go through that door, no one else. Whether you are asking for help, or going to give help, you are the only one who has to deal with problems at the end of the day.

SADDEST MOMENT?

Watching my cousin die of cancer. She was 40. I used to see my aunts and one day they turned up and said my cousin was ill. I went round to see her. My aunt said, 'When you go in and see her, be prepared.' I didn't understand what she meant but when I went in the only thing I recognised was her voice. I hadn't seen her for about three months. Apparently, she'd been ill for a while and I knew she was losing weight. She went from about ten stone to about six stone.

She smiled and said, 'How're you doing?

I said, 'Oh, all right,' but I felt like I'd seen a ghost. I felt all shaky inside like when you've got to go to court in the morning and you know you're going to get a ten-stretch or whatever. That shaky feeling before you get the cold sweats. Like after a big night out.

That was one of the worst experiences of my life because, just before she died, she came to me in a dream and asked me to let her go. I went to see her on the Monday, she came to me in the dream on the Tuesday and she died on the Thursday. It took me about a year to accept the fact that she had gone. I felt ... hopeless. Just hopeless.

WHAT RATTLES YOUR CAGE?

People who are going to do people wrong. Wrong 'uns. People who hurt children. People who scare people like women just walking down the road and they're scared of someone coming up behind them.

I remember, when I was 16, there was this old woman walking down the road and I had to cross the road to make her feel comfortable because I was a black man walking down the road behind her. I knew what she was probably thinking. People who make old people think like that – they annoy me.

I always feel uncomfortable walking behind a woman, I feel I know what they're thinking and I have to make myself aware for them, I have to move that much away from them so they can feel comfortable. I feel it when they're walking towards me so I say excuse me or I walk in the road so they walk on without worrying. That could be my mother, my girlfriend, my daughter.

HAVE YOU EVER REALLY LOVED ANYONE?

Yeah, yeah, yeah, yeah. You can't beat love. Whatever people say about love these days, it's that emotional feeling that comes over you which you can't explain.

Men can't express their feelings, women can. But I've seen men kill themselves over women. I think love is the biggest emotion, it brings men to their knees. I've seen big men top themselves, I've seen big men overdose. I've had big men ring me up on the phone and say, 'I can't handle it no more, I'm going to shoot myself.'

Then I've had to go round his house and spend time with him. I'm in love now and I'm happier than I used to be because I've learned to understand my stupid ways and learned that my way of dealing with things hasn't always been right. So I've learned to look at other angles and listen to what other people say and look at how I am when I'm in a relationship.

I can see what I used to do and I say to myself, 'Let's not do that now, let's have a good time. Let's have a laugh and a joke.' I've mellowed – I guess it comes with age!

WHAT FRIGHTENS YOU?

The fact of knowing that I've got to look over my shoulder when someone says, 'I'm going to come and get yer' – I can't stand that. I think if you're going to come and get someone, do it now because I've got no time to look over me shoulder. If that's the case, then I'll go and do it myself.

I suppose I'm a bit paranoid. Paranoia is paranoia and it does wind you up, but it helps; it helps because it keeps you aware of yourself all the time, keeps you asking questions.

DESCRIBE A HARD BASTARD

A hard person to me is someone who comes up to you and does what he does and then walks away and doesn't say anything about it. That's not using anything, whether it's his hands or fists or whatever. He just comes up to you and gives it to you and that's it. And that can be anyone; doesn't have to be the strongest man in the world, it can be the youngest kid.

NAME A HARD BASTARD

My mum. She is a Born-again Christian now, but when I was younger you didn't wanna mess with her. I would say my mum, then my dad.

WHERE DO YOU SEE YOURSELF IN FIVE YEARS?

Hopefully in the Caribbean, looking after my mum and dad, and settled with my girlfriend. I'll be looking back on my life and thinking I've had a good run.

ANY REGRETS?

No, not really. I wish I'd given a bit more back to my mum. I do regret not getting a better education. I'd like to have learned to read and write a lot better. I should have educated myself a bit more – that's my regret. But I've got my education from people around me.

HARD BASTARD

Baz Allen

BAZ ALLEN

Baz Allen is big, black and he constantly wears a black bowler hat and he reminds me of someone.

'Do you like *The Avengers*?' I ask.

'No, it's more of a James Bond thing,' he grins. 'It's more about me being available anywhere, any time, wherever, whatever. It's Baz for hire. It signifies that I'm a gentleman and a bowler is a British tradition.'

That's it! I've got it! Not Steed – Odd-Job!

Baz is intelligent, charming, witty. He dressed like a City gent and he spoke like a City gent. From his reputation, I suppose I expected a bit of a thug, but he's not like that. He had real manners, he was sophiscated – Odd-Job the Gentleman.

I'd noticed Baz at the endless gansters' dos and book launches I'd been to. He cropped up everywhere. I didn't know anything about him, but then why should I? Then, while researching this book, I was looking through piles of photographs – gansters, villains, hoodlums, tough guys of all shapes and sizes. There, time and time again, was this big black man in the bowler hat.

Who the hell was he? What does he do? Where does he come from? Who was this strange enigma in the bowler? I started to make a few calls.

'Who's the big black man in the smart suit?'

Answer: 'Don't know.'

'The one with a big smile? '

'Don't know.'

'The one with the bowler hat.'

'Oh ... you mean Baz Allen ...'

There is no mistaking Baz Allen and it made the job of finding him easy. Brilliant for me and for this book. But maybe not so good if I was a hitman or, even worse, God forbid, the Old Bill.

NAME : Baz Allen

DATE OF BIRTH : 28 July 1967

STAR SIGN : Leo – and I'm a real Leo, you know you get some people who are like Cancer/Leo, well I'm a Leo Leo. I'm bang in there.

OCCUPATION : Minder/enforcer for the firm. I also work for myself and for a famous Indian family who do hundreds of millions of pounds' worth of business. Say no more!

BACKGROUND

I've been around violence all my life. My father was violent. I watched my father beat my mother up. I used to watch my father beat me up! The first time I remember being violent myself was when I was about six and there was this guy at school called Roy Jackson. He used to agitate me for some reason.

I was a bit over-sensitive and I remember the teacher separating me from him all the time. Then one day we were going home and I caught him on the fire escape. He grabbed me and I pushed him really hard down the stairs and he cracked the side of his head and I thought, Got you, you bastard.

That was the first time that I projected the violence I'd seen from my father on to someone else. It was a release for me. I was a frustrated little kid. When you're that young you can't really explain how you feel but you know you're frustrated. You're stressed out but you can't communicate – you can barely speak. I was like a little tornado!

I went on to the junior school, then the seniors where I got suspended because I got into a fight with a teacher. He'd been picking on my sister – I've got two brothers and two sisters. I was suspended and the next day my parents took me to the school. I was told I had to apologise but I suppose I was being a bit arrogant about it because I refused. So they expelled me. And, of course, my dad gave me a hiding because I'd been expelled.

People say if you get bullied as a child you either

supress your anger or it turns you the other way and I think my behaviour did stem from bullying when I was younger. I'm not making excuses – I'm just analysing it.

LIFE OF CRIME

I went to reform schools. The first thing I got nicked for was pinching milk bottles. All of us kids did it and then we'd go to a friend's house and have a fry-up! I think I got a caution for that.

Then I got pulled over after threatening someone with a knife. I ended up before Highgate magistrates and got a year's conditional discharge. After that I went on to street robberies with my mates, street robberies with tear gas. I got sentenced to three and three concurrent for that. I kept the clipping out of the local newspaper and it read: TERROR FIRM GOES DOWN. Terror firm – we were only about 17!

Then we used to do wage snatches, shops, steaming – we probably started off the steaming in London. We'd be ten or fifteen guys who'd go steaming into stores and we'd have six or seven tills. Then there was burglary, doing a house – I got a 'short, sharp, shock' for that. It started off as GBH then went down to ABH. I came out of that and then did youth custody. Then, after that, no more time. I suppose I got wise. I put myself at the sharp end but when I got involved I was very careful about everything I did.

IS PRISON A DETERRENT?

No.

I heard someone on the TV the other day saying we should give stiffer sentences, the three-strike rule, lock them up, make them work. But if you penalise someone, they rebel. They're not going to cave in and say, 'Oh, I'm never going to prison again.' People come out of prison vicious. They come out and they're nasty. They're more inclined not to leave bodies hanging about. If they go to a house or they go to a bank and it looks like a witness is there – he goes.

You've got to understand the person as well as the crime. You can't just throw huge sentences at them. You've got to show some kind of interest in them when they're in prison. Don't just bang them up or they'll turn to drugs. Education helps – you've got to get people actively involved in something. When you're banged up it's bloody boring. Often people think that drugs is the only way they can get through their sentence. Then they still end up bullying or being bullied. They still end up raping or being raped. It just goes on. There's no change. Prison, as it is, is really no deterrent.

DO YOU BELIEVE IN CAPITAL PUNISHMENT?

Fucking hell. That's a bit coarse, isn't it? What happens if you never did it? What happens if you've been fitted up? It's an injustice and you're gone.

But child molesters ... How do you deal with them? You can't keep locking them up then letting them out, then locking them up. They're filth, these people. I've got two sons, one of six and one of fourteen and, to be honest, if anything happened to them, people would go. You've got to electrocute these people. Just spark them up with a proper lorry battery, know what I mean?

WHAT WOULD HAVE DETERRED YOU FROM A LIFE OF CRIME?

I didn't get much attention shown to me when I was at school because, maybe, I was a bit of a disturbed child. But I was a bright lad, I loved poetry, literature, language.

I just didn't get the attention or encouragement. The teachers didn't have that way of dealing with people. I suppose if we'd had money it would have made a difference.

HAVE YOU EVER BEEN STABBED/SHOT?

I've been shot at. We were doing a recovery somewhere in Epping. Basically, we'd given the guy 48 hours to do something, to come up with the money and he hadn't. We got the sob story, took back what we could, there was 15 grand in the house and we took that and we took his motor.

We were the other side of the A11, not going fast, when his friends appeared and suddenly the back window's gone out. They were obviously drugged up and they started trying to drive us off the road. So, yeah, I've been shot at and it's not as glamorous as you might see it on *Lock, Stock* and all that.

Baz Allen

Stevie Knock

Kevin Chan

Daniel Reece

Chris Murphy

Geoff Thompson

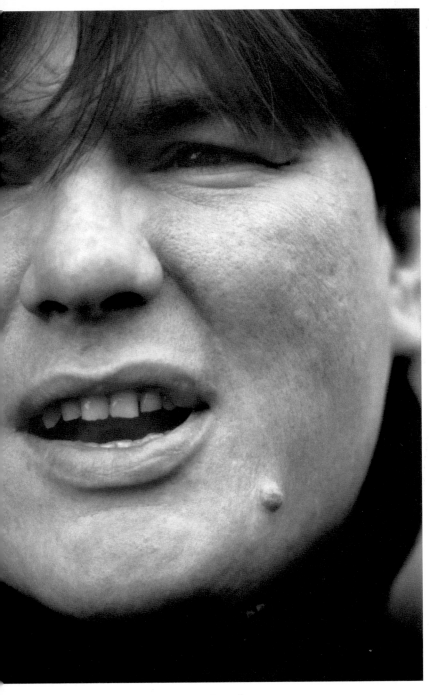

Dave Davis

Jamie O'Keefe

SCARIEST MOMENT?

It's difficult for me to explain without giving too much away, but I'll try … I think that was my scariest moment. And I've been in a situation where someone had … we had … to get someone back. They'd gone off with something. I turned up at the house where they were and this person was hell-bent on saying they didn't have what they had. They kept saying, 'I haven't got it, I haven't got it.'

They got a bit of a hiding and they were still saying they hadn't got it. It was getting to a point where a decision was going to be made and the people who were doing it weren't too solid on what they were doing, if you get my drift.

I wasn't sure whether they were going to end up doing something which would mean everyone getting life. That was a bit of a scary moment then.

SADDEST MOMENT?

My half-brother committed suicide. It was all because of a loving relationship. The girl he had been involved with didn't want him back – he was only in his teens. I've also got a top mate who's doing 20 and his mother was like a second mother to me. I watched her die slowly of cancer. She had breast cancer and they cut it out but it came back. Those are my saddest moments.

WHAT RATTLES YOUR CAGE?

Disrespect. I've been done for road-rage, all kinds of shit and for what? For principles. I'm not rude, I'm polite but disrespect can rev you up.

Racial harassment doesn't really rattle my cage because, to be honest with you, I haven't received that much. Not since I was younger. But I remember when I was just 13 being pulled by the Special Patrol Group. Me and my friend saw a car that had been dumped and it still had the speakers in so we took them. We knew a guy who'd buy them off us.

So we were walking along in our Adidas jackets – we'd both walked into C&A, put them on and walked out again which was the best way to do things in those days – and we were each carrying a speaker.

We bumped into the police. I threw my speaker over the fence but my friend Mike wanted to keep his. A police van pulled up and they put us in the van and I watched as one of the coppers put his gloves on. Suddenly, without warning, he grabbed me and he started to strangle me, I swear to God. He was strangling me and saying, 'Where's the fucking speaker, you black bastard?'

Then they picked up my mate with a truncheon between his legs. They ruptured him, really ruptured him. It was bad. It's frightening when you've got a big bastard like that with big gloves on sitting over you and strangling you and saying, 'Where's the speaker, you black bastard?' I was only 13.

It's violence that's made me violent.

HAVE YOU EVER REALLY LOVED ANYONE?

Yeah. The mother of my second son, I love her to bits. I absolutely love her to bits. She's so beautiful. When I used to work the doors years ago and I'd come in late, she'd be in bed. She'd sit on the end of the bed and rub my feet for me. She'd actually rub my feet while I was asleep. She'd be knackered but she'd still massage my feet. She was lovely. She and I would have our differences and I was young, a bit insecure. I screwed around with another girl and, well, there you go.

She went. Same old, same old ...

WHAT FRIGHTENS YOU?

I suppose what frightens me is what revs me up. Like if a man came on to me in a funny way and I didn't know him and I was in a bar. It might intimidate me for a moment – then I retaliate with anger. I suppose it all stems from when I was younger with my father. If I'm in a difficult situation, I will make up my mind. I'm not frightened. If I have to do something, I'll go over there and do it and it's done – done my way. I don't ever want to be doing life but I understand how easy it is to turn on someone. That's frightening.

DESCRIBE A HARD BASTARD

It's not your doorman standing there staunch with a shaven head saying, 'I'll have yer.' That's not a problem. I'd say a hard bastard is a man who is hard from inside, he's hardened through the years. He has chosen his life and he will stand by his convictions, he will go all the way. It's not there in the exterior of a man. It's inside. It's will he go the extra mile?

NAME A HARD BASTARD

Joey Pyle. He's staunch. He's a lovely geezer but when Joe says it's time, it's time. All the people know that. He's got that respect from people.

WHERE DO YOU SEE YOURSELF IN FIVE YEARS?

Fuck, I hope it isn't in prison. I would like to be a millionaire, I would like to be a celebrity, I'd like to be happily married! I like the finer things in life ... I don't get kicks out of doing the wrong thing but, like I said ... this is a way of life and you choose it as a way of life. If I don't work I don't get paid. I have to be professional and you learn to deal with people in a professional way because that's the way life is. I'm a people person and I get fulfilled in life by what I'm doing now.

ANY REGRETS?

Yeah, fucking that bird when I should have been with my wife. And I'd done a lot of dough for her – credit cards, champagne, hotels, diamond rings, everything. She went off with one of my mates but I could hardly complain because *I* nicked her from one of my mates! And, of course, I should have been with my wife. What goes around, comes around.

Apart from that no regrets, not really. I wrote this poem:

A thief is not a man of shame,
Merely one who advocates from blame.
He seeks the sordid life of crime
His worst nightmare is serving time

He seeks a sort of regal fame
To justify his ill-gotten gain
Heed these words I say so plain
A thief is not a man of shame.

HARD BASTARD

Stevie Knock

STEVIE KNOCK

Stevie Knock is a bouncer extraordinaire. He worked the door for 13 years and he's seen the lot, knows the lot, had more rucks ... you know the score! What Stevie doesn't know about the door isn't worth knowing!

If you're on the door, he says, you know you're going to get trouble sooner or later if you work long enough then you've got to be prepared. What surprised me was that he blames women for a lot of it. It's the women who often kick up, he says. 'They can start a hell of a lot.'

The women start it, then the men with them, as Stevie puts it, 'their mentality does them in. It's the old male bravado. The men finish what the women started ...'

Stevie is big, bloody big. He's training and fitness mad. When he walks into a room he has a presence, an aura. Everything about him is rugged and manly. He hasn't really got a neck – it's as big as his shoulders, it's as if his head has just been plopped on to his shoulders.

Get him talking about the door and suddenly he comes alive. He has story after story of violent encounters, each one more brutal than the last. He leaps to his feet to emphasise what happened during a stabbing; he acts out every detail, not to show off or boast but to make sure I get the story *exactly right*. He has gone, and still would go, toe to toe with any man from here to wherever. He is as tough and brutal as they come.

But ... but ... every man has an Achilles heel and Stevie is no exception.

Just the mere mention of his girlfriend's name turns this big guy to jelly. Julia is the love of his life. His girl, his sweetheart, his friend and confidante. Suddenly, the conversation is no longer about violence, violence, violence. Now it's all top hat and tails, romance, bridesmaids ... Yep, Stevie and Julia are getting married. Will she tame him? We'll see ...

NAME: Stevie Knock

DATE OF BIRTH: 18 February 1967

STAR SIGN: Aquarius

OCCUPATION: Full-time builder, recently retired as a doorman

BACKGROUND

I had two sisters but one died when I was nine and she was eight. That was a big turning point for me. My other sister is still alive, she's youger than me. I was brought up in Bermondsey, we used to live down the Old Kent Road. I had a really difficult childhood. There was no money about. Dad wasn't always there so my mum brought me up alone a lot of the time. Then my sister died and that freaked me out.

I looked like a little angel but I was very, very agressive. I think that came from looking after my sister. She was in and out of hospital for quite a while and it was me mainly looking after her. She had a malignant brain tumour so it affected her slowly; gradually it affected her speech and sight. She wore the national health specs and, kids being kids, she was a prime target for people to have a pop at, so me and my little gang looked after her. I was leader of the gang and I was called Knock-out Knock. It was the milkman who first called me that because I used to help him but then we fell out because I robbed him to pay for our Christmas turkey.

LIFE OF CRIME

I've been arrested numerous times but I've been lucky enough never to go away. There were accusations of violence, a few other things they couldn't prove. I've been lucky.

DO YOU THINK PRISON IS A DETERRENT?

Yes, I do, because I certainly wouldn't like my freedom

taken away from me. I'm a straight guy – ish – but the trouble is when my temper gets the better of me. Normally I'm very straight, very sensible. I know what to do not to get myself into too much trouble. I try and keep two steps in front. My temper is very calculated – I can switch it on and off like a light. My trouble is – and it's a fault of me own – I tend to be too spiteful. My own attitude is that I'll always come out on top. Out of all the hundreds and hundreds of encounters, I've never lost one. Never been knocked down, never. But I've always been fair; anyone's ever hit the deck, I've never followed it up. If he goes down, he can go down and stay there and he stays there on his own.

There was an incident once when I was working the door down the Old Kent Road and I had this Portuguese guy round telling me he was special forces, telling me how tough he was, this, that and the other. But then it got a bit out of hand. He told me I was too big or fat or whatever. When it actually comes to the row, I took his eye out. Because he's told me how tough he was, I've gone in all the way. I don't regret it. I've never in me life regretted anything I've done.

DO YOU BELIEVE IN CAPITAL PUNISHMENT?

I do for certain cases; the obvious one is the kids because they're defenceless so someone's got to really dish it out to these people. I couldn't actually say for all murderers because it's part and parcel.

Some people murder within their business, there are decent criminals. Definitely, it's the children really. Some women ask for it – no, that's a joke! Rapists, I don't know, what do you do with them? I think they should go with the child molesters. No man has the right to do that, to take that.

WHAT WOULD HAVE DETERRED YOU FROM A LIFE OF CRIME?

A very well-paid job. But to get that you'd need a good education and I haven't had the chance. Education, it's the answer to material gains. It's the answer to your everyday life – houses, cars, the way you eat, the way you go out. A good education does give you the basics.

HAVE YOU EVER BEEN STABBED/SHOT?

I've been stabbed twice in the body and cut – I had a very bad cut all around the ear. And I've been shot in the head. That happened when I was on the door. It's part of door work, just one of those things. It was meant for someone else but I happened to be in the way and took the full force of a shotgun. They're still in there now as reminders, there are about 24 shots in there.

But it's part and parcel. At the end of the day, I've dished out some, so what goes around comes around. I couldn't be a liar and a hypocrite and say I didn't do similar.

SCARIEST MOMENT?

When I was told my sister had died, it frightened the life out of me. I didn't know what I was going to do without her.

SADDEST MOMENT?

I was off on a weekend with the Cubs and my dad and my grandad met me off the minibus in the Old Kent Road. They told me my sister had gone into hospital to have an operation for the tumour. They said she was there for the weekend but she didn't come out.

WHAT RATTLES YOUR CAGE?

Disrespect. I've got a lot of respect for people I've met, people like Roy Shaw, people that have got a history. What rattles my cage is these guys who go on and there's no proven history. They make up what they like.

I mean, if I want to talk about my past there's always been someone there to back up what I say.

So disrespect rattles my cage. And bullies. I can't stand a bully, never have done.

HAVE YOU EVER REALLY LOVED ANYONE?

My Julia – we're getting married in August. And my kids.

WHAT FRIGHTENS YOU?

Harm coming to people like my family. That's all. Not myself. Nothing bothers me like that. I'll handle it. I'm only frightened of things I can't control, when I'm not there, things happening to Julia or my family, my kids, mother, father, that sort of stuff.

DESCRIBE A HARD BASTARD

A hard bastard is someone who can have it toe to toe and always, or mainly, come out on top. He's respectful with it. He's just hard, no talk. Someone who can just get on with it, who'll row with anyone and won't pick and choose their victims.

NAME A HARD BASTARD

I think one of the toughest people I know is my mother. It's a different kind of hardness. She's tough because she's had to be, the way she coped when my sister died. She loves kids, she's so good with kids. She's had a bad time with my kids because she has difficulty seeing them as often as my ex-wife has custody of them. That's crushing but she's tough, my mum.

Apart from that, well, I suppose I'm the toughest one I know. I've come against all sorts and I've never shied away from a fight in my life. I just wouldn't – it's not in my nature. I would never go into a fight thinking that I was going to lose. I'm trained in the martial arts. I'm used to full-contact fighting and kick-boxing.

WHERE DO YOU SEE YOURSELF IN FIVE YEARS?

Happily married to Julia and hopefully we'll have our first child. But, still, my principles would be the same – nothing like that will change. I see myself, in five years' time … just happy really.

ANY REGRETS?

I could say about me ex but I won't. I can't have any regrets because if I had regrets I wouldn't be where I am now. So life is what it is. If I regretted things … no … maybe life could have taken a different path. I don't regret anything because things that have happened in my past have shaped my future, and have made me into the man I am today.

HARD BASTARD

Kevin Chan

KEVJN CHAN

He might be called Kevin and he might not look like a man mountain but this is one hard bastard you wouldn't want to mess with because – you'd be for the chop!

Kevin Chan is only 34 but he's a world-famous kung fu instructor and practises something called Wing Chun Kung Fu. It's the kung fu that's been fought for years in the back alleys of Hong Kong and China and was brought to the UK in the Fifties by a man they call the Grand Master Yip Man. He, incidentally, taught the late Bruce Lee.

Kevin is modest – and controlled.

'I like Wing Chun – you use someone's force against them – that's how it works,' he told me.

Kevin is also a ju-jitsu Masters Champion – ju-jitsu is famous for dominating the Ultimate Fighting Championships and other no-holds-barred events.

As I say, you wouldn't want to mess with Kevin. Kevin is suave. Sophisticated. A modern man. A millennium man. He drives a silver Masarati, has a flash London pad on Clapham Common and a riverside house in Portsmouth. He's not a villain, a gangster, a hoodlum – and, *no*, he's not a triad. He's a straight, honourable guy, a man on a mission. He's going places – big time! That was obvious when I met him. It was a refreshing change from the tough guys I usually meet.

On our second meeting I went to the Pineapple Studio to watch him in action. Cor blimey, is he fast! He may be wiry, and one of the smallest men in the book, but he is certainly one of the deadliest ...

NAME: Kevin Chan

DATE OF BIRTH: 11 June 1967

STAR SIGN: Gemini

OCCUPATION: Kung-Fu Master and instructor

BACKGROUND

My family background is Hong Kong Chinese. My family came to the UK in the Sixties to work in Chinese restaurants and take-aways. I was born in Scotland while they worked there. We moved around as a family probably ten times before finally settling down in Portsmouth when I was about 14. I speak English as my main language but I also speak Cantonese Chinese.

I've got one brother and two sisters. Each new move meant going to new schools, and being Chinese meant that we usually stuck out like sore thumbs because there were rarely other Chinese kids there. When you get to a new school, the other kids muck about, they kind of test the waters. Kids being kids used to taunt us to establish their hierarchy in the playground pecking order. So, from a very young age, we learned diplomacy and, if we needed to, we fought.

My career teacher suggested I should work in Mum and Dad's take-away when I left school because, supposedly, I wasn't intelligent enough for anything else! But I got my O-levels and A-levels and went on to University to get a BA Honours in Humanities!

At the time, I was thinking about a career in the Army, so I spent three years in the University of London Officer Training Corps. In the end, I decided it wasn't for me.

I first started kung fu training in Hong Kong when I was 12 and I continued with it when I was back in the UK, studying various styles.

Kung fu is tough but it's so much more than that. It's my job now but I enjoy it so much that, to this day, I feel I've never really worked in my life! More than anything else, the martial arts I do is an intelligence game. In competition, you're not just using muscle and strength, the big guy doesn't always have to win – that's what people want to see and understand when they come to see me in exhibitions. That's what sells.

Kung fu to me is my centre – everything directly or indirectly revolves around it. It is my career, a way of understanding myself, a way to get fit. One of the most important aspects of kung fu I have learned is that using force and aggression in itself can drain and be counter-productive. It is all about using intelligence and using force correctly in a way that's efficient and effective.

LIFE OF CRIME

None. I'm a straight, honourable guy.

DO YOU THINK PRISON IS A DETERRENT?

It depends on the circumstances. I don't think it does act as much of a deterrent. If I did a crime and I had to do time, as long as it wasn't for too long, I would look upon it as a way of developing my own character. I'd read and write a few books, study. I'd use that time out. I wouldn't think of it as a negative thing. There could be a positive side to it – it could be a cloud with a silver lining.

Prison is only a deterrent to some people. The majority of people in prison did not anticipate getting caught. People who are in prison – at least many of them – probably believe in the notion that crime is getting caught, not actually committing it.

HAVE YOU EVER BEEN STABBED/SHOT?

No, nothing like that. Somone has pulled a knife on me but I dealt with it adequately.

SCARIEST MOMENT?

The scariest moments for me are when I run away from myself on certain issues rather than address them directly. I know I'm cowering away and I hate that in myself.

In a situation of confrontation with someone else, I feel quite OK. Usually I walk away. I have done demonstrations when someone wants trouble. I'll always try and deal with it diplomatically. I don't want to get involved to be honest, what's the point? It's all rubbish. I lose either way. If I fight, it means I've lost control. If I don't fight, it looks like I won't fight.

And if the general public are there, I always say to the person, 'Wait behind until I've finished my demonstration. I'll talk to you and answer your questions then.' Usually they don't wait, they wanted to have a go in front of the public, not just me.

Only once has someone actually waited and stayed behind – but then they wouldn't go for it anyway.

My scariest moment didn't actually come from fighting but from surfing! I was in Bali and I ended up surfing one day that can only be described as potentially fatal. No one else was in the water except a handful of really top pros. I only ended up in the water that day because the day before I had cowered away from it. Then the waves had been smaller but I felt I had let myself down.

So I had to take control and face my demons and take 'the drop'. It was a scary experience. The most frightening thing was that everything was totally unpredictable – anything could have happened.

SADDEST MOMENT?

You know what? I can't really recall a specific moment that was so sad it sticks out in my mind. I can't think of a time when any girl's dumped me or whatever. I try to be really positive – difficult times make me stronger.

WHAT RATTLES YOUR CAGE?

When someone takes advantage of my nice nature and confuses being nice with being weak. The other is when I know something is being done half-heartedly. People make excuses or simply cannot be bothered to rectify the situation, hoping I will simply forget or give up.

Also squeaky floorboards – they drive me nuts!

HAVE YOU EVER REALLY LOVED ANYONE?

We're a close family and I love all of them. Some of them I don't see that often, but they know I will always be there for them. I love my parents. They have until recently struggled to make a living, working 14 hours a day, seven days a week. They went without holidays to put clothes on our backs and give us a better life. Now that they are in their autumn years, I hope I can give them as much love and support as they have given us.

DESCRIBE A HARD BASTARD

What makes a hard bastard? You've got to be adaptable, got to be flexible. Hard bastards, really hard bastards, are very low key. Fighting for fighting's sake is pointless. What are you going to achieve from it? I don't really admire people in that respect. I understand that some people who have no education have got to work in the black economy and I understand that and what goes with it. But these tin-pot gangs who go around shooting one another, they're trying to make a reputation for themselves which I don't admire. What's the point of using force like that?

I like martial arts because it helps me to understand myself, my strengths and weaknesses. Sometimes people take up kung fu because they've been bullied at school or picked on so they learn some crazy moves because they think it will help. They haven't got confidence in themselves so they think they will get it from something else.

But they're going for it the long way round. They think, I'll learn kung fu, that will really make me hard, I can knock him out, or whatever.

But you don't learn kung fu for that. If you really want to take someone out, and that's the reason you're doing it, you do it by other means.

Kung fu makes you understand yourself. You've got to be dedicated. For me, it's my life, my work, my business.

If you are too hard, you are brittle. I believe in being adaptable, flexible and being able to totally mould yourself around your opponent to limit his options. Successful hard bastards will only use the correct amount of pressure for the given situation. They can see that violence is not the only means to an end, it is only the extreme means in an uncompromising situation.

NAME A HARD BASTARD

When I was studying in London and I joined the officer training school I met a lot of people. During that time, I went on attachment and met the SAS and people like that.

They are hard bastards but it's very low key and I like that. They don't go around being violent to prove a point. Those are the kind of people I admire.

Otherwise, my heroes are people like Alexander the Great, conquerors who fought not just for glory or for material gain. They led from the front, showed courage and compassion when needed and so earned the respect of their men.

WHERE DO YOU SEE YOURSELF IN FIVE YEARS?

My kung fu schools already have the largest membership around for such an organisation. I want to continue to work to build standards. I want to elevate the art of Kamon Wing Chun Kung Fu. I really enjoy teaching and helping people to achieve their goals through the martial arts, for self-defence or just to become physically fitter. It is important to me that the people on my courses succeed. I really believe in the win–win–win formula; if you do well, I do well and the organisation does well.

ANY REGRETS?

I regret not trying hard enough in the past when I've been attempting to achieve certain goals. But there's a plus side to that, too – it makes me more aggressive in pursuit of my goals now.

HARD BASTARD

Daniel
Reece

DANJEL REECE

Danny Reece was accused, and found guilty, of murder. He's now serving life in Whitemoor Prison, Cambridgeshire.

He's also been accused of being a grass. He pleads guilty – with mitigating circumstances.

You, the reader, be the jury and decide.

On a tape he sent to me, he tried to put the record straight once and for all.

He was on a prison landing when a 60-year-old lifer called Ronnie Easterbrook hissed, 'So you're the grass?'

It takes a brave man to stand toe to toe with Danny Reece; all the cons feared Danny. Everyone was aware when he was on the landing. Nobody approached him, or had eye contact with him, let alone insult him by calling him a grass.

So when Ronnie Easterbrook arrived and made his accusation, everyone noticed how he didn't move out of the way or avert his eyes. Ronnie had obviously heard about Danny. His sheer size and strength made him unmistakable.

'So you're the grass?'

A breathless hush swept across the landing.

Danny later told me, 'I felt my blood boil; the palms of my hands began to sweat. I looked into the face of a 60-year-old man who dared to call me a grass. A fucking grass. Being called a grass is the worst insult anyone can give you.

'Everyone on the landing expected me to go berserk, but I didn't – I decided to tell Ronnie Easterbrook the truth like I'm telling you. The man involved was a murdering rapist called Dave Lashley.

'Yeah, I suppose you could call me a grass if you count taking a dirty, rotten, filthy nonce off the streets for the rest of his natural life. The way I saw it was that it could have been my mother, sister or daughter that he'd raped and murdered. I felt I had to do something.

'At the time, I was in Brixton Prison in South London. I was given a job in the woodmill and was allowed to train in the gym twice a week. It was there that I met Dave Lashley, a huge black man who was as strong as an ox. We worked together, trained together and had a laugh. I didn't know what Dave was in for and I didn't ask – it's not the done thing.

'It was just another Tuesday morning and a screw had loaned me a copy of the *Sun*.

'The headline screamed out: BLACK RAPIST JAILED FOR TEN YEARS.

'Dave read the headline. "Ten years," he scoffed. "He should have killed the bitch, he wouldn't have got any more time."

'I couldn't believe what I was hearing.

' "The fucking rapist," he went on. "I killed my bitches. He raped one and got the same as me. The mug."

'For once I was speechless. This man was a rapist, a murdering, fucking rapist and I'd been knocking about with him. Before I could say anything, Dave grabbed my head, his huge hands held my skull.

' "This is how I done the bitches," and he began to demonstrate how he killed by pushing his fist into my windpipe. That's when I snapped. I hit him so hard it lifted him off the ground. As he flew backwards, the screws pushed the panic button but it was too late, I was on top of him. I really lost it.

'By the time they pulled me off him, both of us were covered in blood. They assumed the blood was mine until they discovered a big piece of black flesh still in my mouth.

'I testified against him in St Alban's Crown Court and the rapist received a natural life sentence. So yeah, I grassed – on a rapist.

'Unfortunately, in prison, things are exaggerated and every time the story is told it gets bigger and bigger. I've even been accused of grassing on Linda Calvey – the woman I love, my own wife!

'What I've said here is the truth. I've put the record straight. Believe it, if you want to; if you don't, then fuck ya ...'

NAME: Daniel Reece

DATE OF BIRTH: 24 June 1956

STAR SIGN: Cancer

OCCUPATION: Robber

BACKGROUND

I've lived in East London for most of my life. I was born within the sound of Bow Bells in Mile End, Bow, which makes me a Cockney.

All I ever wanted was to be like my Uncle George. He was my boyhood hero. I never knew my dad when I was growing up – he gave my mum seven kids then fucked off. I'm the eldest of the seven – I have three sisters and three brothers. Mum did her best for us but quite often we only just had enough to eat.

We lived in an old pre-fab in Manor Road, Stratford. 'The Round House' we called it – it was just like a dome with two bedrooms at the back, a small kicthen, a sitting room-cum-diner in the front and an outside toilet. There was no electricity or gas so Mum cooked on an open fire.

Bringing up seven children obviously took its toll on Mum and she fell seriously ill. This was the early Fifties. Social Services were called in and they wanted to put us into care but Mum's sisters stepped in and the family, us kids, were split up.

I went off to live with Aunt Maud and Uncle George in Leytonstone in East London. I loved it from the start. George took me everywhere with him. He owned a scrap yard and I used to watch him throw car engines across the yard like they were cardboard boxes. I used to search cars for lost money which I kept.

George always had time for me and I wanted to be strong and respected just like him. Maud became like a second mum to me and I loved them both.

When Mum recovered from her illness, we had to go back to the pre-fab. I didn't want to go – I dreaded it. I had experienced living in a proper house with gas and electric; going back to that poxy pre-fab was the last thing I wanted to do. I had to take drastic action. Things are simple when you're young – in my mind, if the pre-fab wasn't there, then the problem would be solved ... if we didn't have the pre-fab, the Council would have to rehouse us in a proper house just like Uncle George and Auntie Maud. So I went berserk, smashed the windows, ripped doors off hinges, smashed down walls. I totally destroyed the pre-fab. I wasn't caught. My plan worked. The Council were forced to rehouse us.

LIFE OF CRIME

My first court appearance, when I was young, was for criminal damage – I was caught smashing up the toilets in Stratford Station.

Then there was Approved School, then Detention Centre, then prison. Crime goes in steps. You could liken it to an apprenticeship. It starts with small-time thieving, then it progresses to bigger jobs, then the big time, with the odd bit of malicious damage and grievous bodily harm thrown in for good measure until you reach the ultimate goal: armed robberies and murder.

I've been a criminal all my life. I've spent over 20 years in jail for armed robbery and violence. At the moment, I'm serving life for murder.

IS PRISON A DETERRENT?

No.

Prison used to be a simple place. You served your time, deprived of your freedom, living to rules and regulations that dominated your every hour. But prison today is a far cry from simple. It is full of drugs and people connected with drugs, people who live by drugs and for drugs. The drug tests are a complete waste of time and money; they achieve nothing but have created a prison system which is supposedly there to correct but in reality it corrupts.

Heroin is expensive and very addictive. Consequently, the young kids are constantly in debt and are forced into prostitution to pay for their habit. I wish people would understand the stupidity of drugs. The only way out of any situation is to face up to it, confront it, acknowledge it – and change it.

DO YOU BELIEVE IN CAPITAL PUNISHMENT?

Child killers should be put down the same as rabid dogs.

WHAT WOULD HAVE DETERRED YOU FROM A LIFE OF CRIME?

Nothing would have stopped me from a life of crime – it was what I wanted.

HAVE YOU EVER BEEN STABBED/SHOT?

I've been stabbed five times. Shot – no.

SCARIEST MOMENT?

Watching my sons being born.

SADDEST MOMENT?

The death of my son John – it was complete hell.

WHAT RATTLES YOUR CAGE?

Petty people – and people that don't keep their promises. In prison, you meet the very worst sort of human being imaginable and bullies are ten-a-penny. I despise bullies; all bullies are cowards and hide behind the fear they instil in others. But confront a bully and he usually turns into a coward.

HAVE YOU EVER REALLY LOVED ANYONE?

Apart from my sons and my sister's daughter, Tania, I've loved Jennifer, my lovely wife Linda and a little Gremlin.

My future is with Linda, every day and every night I think of her and I write to her every day. I am able to speak to her every fortnight and, if I'm lucky, I get an hour but sometimes it is only for ten minutes.

WHAT FRIGHTENS YOU?

No human being frightens me – I suppose love frightens me the most.

DESCRIBE A HARD BASTARD

Someone that never gives up. Someone who believes in blood for blood and always gets his revenge.

NAME A HARD BASTARD

Ronnie Easterbrook – the only man I've given 100 per cent respect to. The Colonel and Ken Pugh.

WHERE DO YOU SEE YOURSELF IN FIVE YEARS?

I see myself lying on some exotic beach with my dream girl, counting my millions – or maybe playing in the fields of heaven with my son John.

ANY REGRETS?

Not meeting Ronnie Easterbrook 20 years ago – what fun we would have had! And not being there to pick up my son from school.

HARD BASTARD

Chris Murphy

CHRJS MURPHY

**Chris Murphy is The Quiet Man, strong, silent ...
He's a dangerous mother******.**

Chris became part of this book by pure accident. I'd
just finished an interview with Dave Davies. Afterwards,
he went one way and I went the other. An hour later, my
phone rang. Dave had bumped into his old buddy Chris
Murphy in his local off-licence. He hadn't seen him for
donkey's years. Then he told me about his reputation. He
is The Man, he said. I admit, I was intrigued.

I met Chris in a pub in Essex, and instantly knew what
Dave meant. While he chatted, Chris smiled a lot – but
never with his eyes. He never came across as mad – just
slightly unhinged. I felt Chris had more depth to him than
he was letting on. He was secretive about what he did and
how he did it. There was something about him,
something I couldn't put my finger on. After spending a

couple of hours in his company, I was wiser – but not much.

What is his profession? Gangster? Security? SAS?

Whatever he is, he ain't letting on. And I ain't asking ...

Well, of course I did – but decorator? Decorator, my arse!

NAME: Chris Murphy

DATE OF BIRTH: 9 October 1956

STAR SIGN: Libra

OCCUPATION: Decorator

BACKGROUND

I'm an Essex boy. I've got a younger brother and a sister.

That's all I want to say about my background.

LIFE OF CRIME

I've been away. Two years, one year, I did a four-stretch for malicious intent. Violence. The last one was six months for having weapons.

DO YOU THINK PRISON IS A DETERRENT?

I don't know. To some it might be but, in general, no. It's a learning process. For youngsters, I think it might be a deterrent but when you're older, no.

DO YOU BELIEVE IN CAPITAL PUNISHMENT?

Under certain circumstances, yeah. Nonces, people like that, definitely. I'd like to fucking do it.

WHAT WOULD HAVE DETERRED YOU FROM A LIFE OF CRIME?

I don't think anything would have deterred me. Some things are meant to be. I'm not a nine-to-five person, I never could hold down a normal job. I realised that when I was about 15 years old and helping my old man in the building trade. It was fucking hard work and I don't like that! I suppose that's why most people get into crime – why go out working hard for five or even seven days a week when you can make the same amount of money in half-an-hour?

So why bother?

HAVE YOU EVER BEEN STABBED/SHOT?

Yes. Both. I was shot in the leg when I was 20. And I've been stabbed five times. The stabbings happened when I was working on the door when I was younger – the shooting was something else, something I would rather not go into. How does it feel when you're shot? It hurts! But it's strange, you know straight away you've been shot but you don't feel immediate pain, it comes on a few seconds later and you're thinking, Fuck, I've been shot. And the speed of that bullet, when it hits you it burns you.

I've been trained in the use of most small firearms and some other weapons and I know what they can do. But we won't go into that either! I've also trained for years in the martial arts, karate and the Korean martial arts. Your mind is your most dangerous weapon. I always weigh up situations – I never go into anything hot, never.

SCARIEST MOMENT?

I got stabbed when I was abroad, miles from anywhere and no one around to help. That was scary because you don't know what's coming on top at the time. I thought I was going to die … well, I thought I was dead. I was stabbed in the back. It feels like someone's punching you but as soon as that knife comes out you know. If they left the fucker in there, that's all right – but when they take it out, that's what hurts.

When I was stabbed, I couldn't move and I had trouble breathing. That was scary – fighting for breath.

SADDEST MOMENT?

My wife killed herself in 1995 – and she meant to do it. We'd split up about a week before; we'd been arguing a lot, usual things. I picked up my son and took him swimming then dropped him back and I told him to go and see where Mum was, so he went upstairs and said, 'She's asleep on the bed.' So I said, 'Don't wake her – tell her I'll come back later on, pick you up and take you for a meal and that.'

About three hours later, I called my daughter. She told me, 'Mummy's dead.'

What I didn't realise is that she was already dead when I dropped my son off. She'd already shot herself. So my son was in the house on his own with her for four hours. He was only ten at the time. He didn't have a clue because she was lying on her side with a pillow over her – she'd shot herself through the pillow. It looked like she was asleep but she'd shot herself through the heart with one of my guns!

WHAT RATTLES YOUR CAGE?

Rudeness. I don't see any reason for rudeness in people – politeness doesn't cost you anything.

WHAT FRIGHTENS YOU?

My mum! Every time I go round there she finds me another job to do.

DESCRIBE A HARD BASTARD

Hardness comes from years – not how big you are. It all comes from up here – it's all in the mind.

NAME A HARD BASTARD

Roy Shaw. A man not to be messed with.

WHERE DO YOU SEE YOURSELF IN FIVE YEARS?

I'd like to move abroad. I'd like to live in Malta. I like the Maltese people. I'd like it if my daughter wanted to come, too, but it's up to her; she's grown up now – she's got a kiddie of her own. But that would be nice – us all together out there in the sun.

ANY REGRETS?

Yeah, getting caught! I haven't retired as such but let's say I'm winding down … I think you have to realise after a certain amount of time that you aren't as young as you were, all that kind of thing. I think you realise when you're older that a lot of the things that you argued about when you were younger just aren't worth arguing about. I do think as you get older you definitely get wiser. You think about things a bit more.

What you do think about is the consequences, the repercussions of your actions as you get older. When you're young you don't give a toss. Getting five or ten at that age – getting five or ten at my age is something entirely different, know what I mean?

When you're older, you've settled down, you've got the house and all that; you don't want to give it up. Inside, you've got three meals a day, a roof over your head … in many ways, it's worse for the people you love on the outside. Even so, I don't want to go back to that.

HARD BASTARD

Geoff
Thompson

GEOFF THOMPSON

Geek, nerd, wuss ...

Wrong, wrong, wrong. What you see is *not* always what you get.

Geoff Thompson is the most unlikely-looking hard bastard I've ever seen. But don't be fooled. Beneath his nylon shirt and Crimpolene slacks lies an awesome power.

You only have to read his book to know that he has been through the mill and back again.

Geoff was the only tough guy to bring me chocolates when I met him. He was chatty, witty and the perfect gent, not at all the bruiser that I'd heard about. I began to wonder if I had the right Geoff Thompson.

It made me question what a hard bastard is supposed to look like and act like. All our preconceived ideas are of a man who can lift a ton but can't spell it! You imagine shaven heads and tattoos.

But Geoff is living proof that tough guys come in all shapes and sizes; colours, creeds and age are immaterial.

It might sound sexist, but I think every man has the potential to be dangerous. Geoff Thompson is no exception, but he has used his experiences in a positive way. He has written 30 books on the subject of violence. He has written plays and film scripts, he's even published his own books. He's been there, done it.

So don't be fooled by his manner and his niceness. Someone once told me, 'Only a fool takes kindness as weakness ...' That someone was Ronnie Kray.

NAME: Geoff Thompson

DATE OF BIRTH: 26 April 1960

STAR SIGN: Taurus

OCCUPATION: Writer

BACKGROUND

When I was younger, I suffered from depression, I was in fear – fear of life really. One day, I got so tired of being fearful and depressed I thought I've got to do something about it, so I sat down and drew a pyramid on a piece of paper and I wrote out all my fears, one by one. Then I confronted them systematically one by one. And at the top of the fear list was fear of violent confrontation. So I became a doorman to confront my demons. You've just got to be careful when you face the dragon that you don't become the dragon yourself. I went on the door for my own salvation but, once I was on the door, I became the dragon, hugely violent and I started using violence which didn't solve the problem at all.

If someone came into my world, I used violence to knock them back out of it again. I became a person I didn't like. I changed. My mum noticed a change in me and my first wife noticed a change in me. I couldn't see it at the time – it was a gradual realisation.

People started queuing up to fight me. I was eleven-and-a-half stone, I was polite and I had the audacity to be articulate on the dance-room door and I apologised if I couldn't let anyone in – so everyone wanted to fight me. The problem was, although I was in control of the fear, I was still frightened, so if people wanted to confront me I'd knock them out. I didn't like the feeling of the pre-fight, I didn't like the feeling of the fight itself, I only liked the feeling of the post-fight because the endorphins in my body were racing.

I'd have a man on the floor and I'd kick him like a coconut. It wasn't gratuitous, it was because I was frightened to death, frightened he was going to beat me because there was a part of me inside that was still a nine-stone weakling saying, 'I can't believe I've knocked him down. I'm not going to leave it so he can get up again.'

Especially the people I was dealing with – gang members and such like. It wasn't that I was brave, it was just that I didn't want him to get up and fight me again. I didn't want him to come back and fight me the next day. So, most of my violence came from insecurity.

But as I've grown and become more confident, I've let the violence go. So I don't look at violent people and see bravery – I see insecurity. That's what martial arts does for you. I want to be so good at what I do, so confident about what I do, that I can just walk away. Even though someone might not know that I've let them off, I will let them off. Martial arts teaches you how to kill people – but once you know, there's not a single part of you that wants to do it. That's where my real strength is. I can walk away with confidence.

When you're violent, you dehumanise people – if you're kicking someone like a coconut, you can't see them as a husband or a son. They're no longer human in your eyes. But if you learn martial arts, you learn about yourself, you don't have to walk about posturing. People who really know how to take care of themselves are gentle people. I admire that and I admire intelligence.

I was in my mid-twenties when I realised. I'd suffered from anxiety, depression and fear most of my life on and off. I realised that I wasn't really frightened of people, I was frightened of feelings. I had to live with those feelings. Now I still don't like it, but I can live with it – that comes with experience.

LIFE OF CRIME

I've never been a criminal or a gangster – I was a doorman.

DO YOU THINK PRISON IS A DETERRENT?

I don't think the present system is fantastic – I think prison should be tied in with some kind of educational programme.

Obviously you need some system which is punishment, but if we're going to send people to prison, while they're in there they should be somehow motivated and inspired to change. If people have got the skill and the bottle to make a living from crime, they can make a living from anything – they need to be shown that. It's a question of changing direction.

DO YOU BELIEVE IN CAPITAL PUNISHMENT?

No, I don't. I don't really believe in blood for blood. If someone commits a crime, they go to jail – that is the consequence of their actions. I think once you start killing people, you become them. But there's a paradox here because I would be prepared to kill somebody if my own survival was at stake.

But I wouldn't class that as violence – that's survival. If you've done everything possible in a violent confrontation to get out of the situation, but you find your own survival is at stake, that's different. You are then defending yourself. That's natural law. But capital punishment, you're killing someone in a cold-blooded way – I wouldn't want to do it, I wouldn't want to put my hand to it. I think you punish people more when you put them in prison for the rest of their lives than when you kill them.

WHAT WOULD HAVE DETERRED YOU FROM A LIFE OF CRIME?

It was a growing realisation that violence doesn't work – so I started to try not to be violent. So, when I was working the doors, I tried to solve all the problems by communicating, by talking. It didn't always work.

There was one particular guy who was trouble but I tried to talk him down. Unfortunately, he mistook my politeness for weakness and over three months he just got more and more rude. We ended up having a fight in the car park. I knocked him down first punch but I was so angry, all the anger of three months came out and I just destroyed him. I couldn't control my anger. I thought I'd killed him – I hadn't – but in my mind I had. Everybody gathered round and there were people saying, 'He's dead, he's dead.' They took him off to hospital and I remember driving home; it was a lonely drive home, and I was thinking, I'm going to go to prison.

I got home and my wife was in bed asleep and the kids were asleep and I looked at them and they were so beautiful. It was as if a veil dropped from my eyes, it was like a film, and I thought, I'm losing her, I'm losing them and for what?

So I stopped working on the door and I started writing books. That was the turning point for me. I just realised that I was risking so much by behaving as I was.

HAVE YOU EVER BEEN STABBED/SHOT?

I got slashed about half-a-dozen times when I was working at a club in Coventry – but that was a big gang fight. A whole gang of them came in on a stag night and the whole place exploded, it got destroyed, glass everywhere – there was about £3,000 worth of broken glass. I got wounds in my head and in my hands. I went down but I kept getting up. But if I'd gone down and stayed down, I think I would have died that night.

SCARIEST MOMENT?

That fight I had with the guy in the car park. That was my scariest moment. It wasn't that I was afraid of being hurt. I was more scared of losing my liberty, my wife and kids. Physical hurt you can deal with, it's the internal hurt that's worse.

SADDEST MOMENT?

Losing my first wife and kids. My first wife was a good girl but we got married when we were 17 and as we grew up we became two different people. Then after we split up, I was in social Siberia – I was in a bedsit and that's all I had, the bedsit. That was the hardest time. I love my kids and I'd always been with them. Leaving the marital home was the hardest thing I ever did. I don't regret it. I had to do it. But it was hard.

WHAT RATTLES YOUR CAGE?

Prejudice. I love colours, I love the different cultures, I love the diversity. I don't like people who judge other people just on the grounds of colour or whatever. I don't think any of us have got the right to judge other people like that.

HAVE YOU EVER REALLY LOVED ANYONE?

Yeah, the lady I'm with now – Sharon. She's my whole life. I love her so much I can't tell you. I can write it down but I can't get it out. She's my soul-mate and I love her so very much. When I met her, I had such an overwhelming feeling of love and I think that's what God must be – that feeling. I don't see God as an old man with a beard, I see God as every living thing, I see God as love, I see God as that feeling.

DESCRIBE A HARD BASTARD

My description of a hard bastard isn't very nice. A hard bastard isn't someone who can just have a fight, a hard bastard is someone that is hard through and through. He's hard with his kids, he's hard with his wife, he's hard with everybody. If I had to describe it in one word, I'd say it was someone who was unhappy. It's not someone I want to be. If someone said I was a hard bastard, I'd feel I had failed. Being hard isn't good. Hardiness is good, by which I mean you can cope with pain.

NAME A HARD BASTARD

Some of the characters in Charles Dickens' books are hard bastards. Scrooge was a hard bastard. He was hated – hard bastards are hated.

WHERE DO YOU SEE YOURSELF IN FIVE YEARS?

I see myself as a West End playwright with my own film showing at a nearby cinema. I see myself happy with my wife and my kids working for me in my publishing company. I see myself really happy in five years.

ANY REGRETS?

I can't regret anything. I'm the living manifestation of everything that's ever happened to me and if I changed anything now I wouldn't be the person I am now.

I wish I hadn't hurt people, but if I hadn't hurt people no one would listen to me now when I say don't hurt people. So no, no regrets.

HARD BASTARD

DAVE
DAVIS

DAVE DAVIS

Early evening in an Essex pub. Dave Davis – D to his friends – is leaning on the bar. It's his round. Holding a crisp £50 note, he asks with a nod, 'What yer 'avin?'

He is 32 years old, broadly built, dressed in a navy suit, a no-nonsense, up-front, in-your-face kinda guy.

He handed me my drink without looking at me. In fact, throughout the interview, he hardly glanced in my direction. If he wasn't talking out of the corner of his mouth on his mobile phone, then he was acknowledging shifty-looking characters with a nod.

Dave Davis is a man's man. That's obvious. He's also one of those men in a hurry – things to do, people to see, places to go. He keeps his cards close to his chest, he gives little away. He was very careful about what he said – and how he said it. A man of few words.

'Don't say much, do you?' I said.

He smiled and, for the first time, looked at me, really looked at me. His blue eyes went straight through me and he whispered, 'Why use two words when one will do?'

But then he started to talk ...

NAME: **Dave Davis**

DATE OF BIRTH: **14 April 1969**

STAR SIGN: **Aries**

OCCUPATION: **Security adviser**

BACKGROUND

I've spent most of my life in Essex. My uncle is Davey Hunt, a well-respected man in Essex. I've got a brother and a sister.

I was a bit of a rogue when I was growing up – I couldn't take authority very well, school and all that, I just didn't like being there. I didn't get on with the other kids that well.

LIFE OF CRIME

I've done time – for violence. I served two out of four when I was 19. That gave me a quick shock and I haven't been back since.

IS PRISON A DETERRENT?

No, not really. Because if you're going to do it, you're

going to do it anyway. If you start thinking about things, it's going to hurt you rather than just getting on and doing it. Now I'm older, prison is more of a deterrent, but when I was younger, no, it wasn't. It's not so much your age, it's when you've got kids of your own – you've got to think of them. They slow you down. Who's going to get them their bread and butter? It makes you more sensible.

DO YOU BELIEVE IN CAPITAL PUNISHMENT?
Mainly no, but for child rapes, all that kind of thing, it goes without saying, doesn't it? Yes.

WHAT WOULD HAVE DETERRED YOU FROM A LIFE OF CRIME?
Lots of money, having wealthy parents. I wouldn't get up and do what I do every day if I had loads of money to burn.

HAVE YOU EVER BEEN STABBED/SHOT?
Yeah, I've been cut, stabbed and I've been shot.

SCARIEST MOMENT?
I haven't really had a scary moment – they come afterwards when you think back on what's happened and you think, That was a bit lively.

In fact, the scariest moment really was when my kids were born; I could hardly stay in the same hospital. I went white and I was having panic attacks. I was frightened, I had to go.

Then I came back when the baby was born and then I

had to go again. Now I've got three little girls and a boy – he's only seven months. I didn't see any of them being born – I just couldn't. Seeing a woman in labour with your child is the scariest thing in the world.

SADDEST MOMENT?

I lost my dad about five weeks ago. My saddest moment ever – still playing on me now. It was a brain tumour. He was only 50. He was governor round this manor. It's been a terrible, terrible shock.

He complained of headaches for three days, went to work, fell asleep in the cab of a lorry and never woke up again. I don't think I will ever get over his death. He wasn't just my dad – he was my best mate. I'm devastated.

WHAT RATTLES YOUR CAGE?

West Ham upset me! But, seriously, paedophiles, people who don't treat their kids right – that really upsets me. Nothing much else.

HAVE YOU EVER REALLY LOVED ANYONE?

My mum and dad. My kids. I don't feel the same for any woman as I feel when I hold my beautiful daughters in my arms or my baby boy. I've never felt such love as the love I feel for them.

DESCRIBE A HARD BASTARD

A hard bastard is a man who's fearless. He doesn't have to be a hard bastard as such – just fearless, scared of nothing.

NAME A HARD BASTARD

My mother, Stephanie. She's fearless.

WHERE DO YOU SEE YOURSELF IN FIVE YEARS?

I can see us in a little house – out of the way so no one could find me, out in the sticks somewhere, comfortably off, retired – but I suppose I've retired already! I've done the door since I was 17 but I've stopped doing it now, so that's retirement.

ANY REGRETS?

No. If a man regrets his past, then he regrets his life. So, no, I've no regrets.

HARD BASTARD

Jamie
O´Keefe

JAMJE O'KEEFE

'Personally, I would be a very happy man if I never get into another fight in my life. It really pisses me off when someone forces me along the path of violence but I am also not able to turn the other cheek and find forgiveness.

'If somebody hurts a member of my family, I would not think twice about unleashing every nasty form of painful application that I know of. Don't get me wrong – I'm not a monster. If you spill my beer in a pub I would not consider that to be something worth fighting for.

'If you road-rage me, I still do not consider it something worth fighting for. However, change the scenario and road-rage me while I have children in the car ... then I would not hesitate to come tearing through your street door at 5.00am and break every bone in your body before you even wipe the sleep from your eyes. I've done that a few times when it was deserved ...'

So writes Jamie O'Keefe in his book *Thugs, Mugs and Violence* – 'Forget the movies, this is the real world' it says on the cover.

Jamie is a man of words, the author of numerous books on self-protection. Apart from *Thugs*, he's written *Old School, New School – A Guide to Bouncers*. Then there's *Dogs Don't Know Kung-Fu*, a female guide to self-protection and *Pre-emptive Strikes for Winning Fights*, the alternative to 'grappling'.

What makes Jamie unusual is that he has published them all himself. And I've got to take my hat off to him. If there was an award for trying, then Jamie wins it hands down. He knows what he's talking about, too. A former doorman through the late Seventies, the Eighties and Nineties, he's living proof that not all doormen are meat-heads.

Yes, Jamie can lift a ton – and spell it. Power to you Jamie. Go, Jamie, – go!

NAME: Jamie O'Keefe

DATE OF BIRTH: 29 April 1961

STAR SIGN: Taurus

OCCUPATION: Author of self-protection books; social care worker for young people with challenging behaviour

---

BACKGROUND

These days, I work with young kids – help them to try and get back on track. When I was about eight years old, a close family member was sexually abused by my dad and I was told about it and you just imagine what it's like dealing with all that information at that age, knowing your dad's a nonce.

So I set fire to our house which was on an estate in Bethnal Green. I was confused. The house felt unclean and I didn't know what to do with it because of my dad. I burned the house down. Then the police got involved and my dad got sent down for what he did. Me and my sister got sent to Scotland to live with our nan for safety's sake. Then we came back and lived in Dagenham and started life again. Then my mum got involved with someone else and he became my stepfather. I've never seen my real father since the day I set fire to the house.

LIFE OF CRIME

None. The nearest I got to it was when the police paid me a visit when Frank Warren, the promoter, got shot, and I was training the guy who allegedly shot him, but who was rightly acquitted. Also, I was a legally licensed firearms holder. But they quickly found out my guns weren't connected in any way. No, even working the door I've never been prosecuted for anything or been sent away.

IS PRISON A DETERRENT?

It depends on what sort of crime you were thinking of committing. I think most people who are committing robberies think they're going to get away with it. For them, prison is no deterrent. I don't think prison is a deterrent to people like paedophiles either, because they don't think they're doing wrong. I think if you've committed just one crime and you go to prison, you probably end up learning more inside than you would outside on the street. So, it doesn't really seem to work, does it?

DO YOU BELIEVE IN CAPITAL PUNISHMENT?

I do believe in capital punishment, but it does worry me that there are sometimes miscarriages of justice and it all goes wrong. Even so, I think there should be capital punishment for sexually-related crimes, paedophiles and rape. For murder, it depends so much on the circumstances. I have a friend doing life for murder – he stabbed someone – but that really was in self-defence. This guy, he's lost his life, the young guy lost his life, all in the space of a few seconds.

I think capital punishment should be there, each judged on the facts of the case, and it should be by lethal injection. I don't believe in hanging. That's gory. It makes us as bad as them to watch someone suffering.

WHAT HAS DETERRED YOU FROM A LIFE OF CRIME?

My stepfather who brought me up was into crime all the time. We used to have to go to visit him in prison. He did all sorts and if I'd followed him I would have gone down. But because he used to beat me up when I was a kid, I didn't get that close to him. He also used to beat my mum up; he used to beat the shit out of her and because I was a skinny little kid I couldn't do anything much about it. So I learned martial arts. I wanted to build myself up so I could kill him. That was the intention – I mean, I used to watch him smash her head against the mantelpiece. This was when I was about ten until I was fifteen.

So I started judo when I was about 12 and went on from there to karate, kick-boxing and kung fu. Then, as I became stronger, he became weaker and more frail and he knew I could have bashed him if I'd wanted to. At the same time, I had in a strange way become attached to him – when he died when I was in my thirties I cried my eyes out.

In his last year, he was in a wheelchair and he wasn't able to hurt anybody, he was that ill. It was terrible what he did to my mum and they were divorced at the end, but without that upbringing I wouldn't have learned all I did and I wouldn't have gone into martial arts so, in a funny way, he helped me … he kept me from following him into crime.

The upbringing he gave me moulded me, it made me streetwise.

HAVE YOU EVER BEEN STABBED/SHOT?

I've been stabbed three times and cut. It was at a club in Canning Town – I've also been shot at by another doorman in my own garden with my own gun! We had a disagreement. He was into drugs and I'm not into drugs; he let me down one night on the door and I got badly beaten up. He came round my house to sort things out and guns and knives and things were out at the time. He raised one of my guns to my head in the garden and pulled the trigger. It was empty but ... after that I got rid of my guns.

SCARIEST MOMENT?

It was when I was at a club. Four or five men got my head down on the pavement and caved my face in, and then threw me over the bridge where the railway lines are. At the time I was petrified. There wasn't much I could do. Two held me down, one stamped on my face and the others were holding my legs.

SADDEST MOMENT?

When my mum died last September. Also my divorce. Losing the kids. That was sheer hell.

WHAT RATTLES YOUR CAGE?

Anyone harming weak people. I hate to see injustice being done.

HAVE YOU EVER REALLY LOVED ANYONE?

Yes, once. She knows who she is.

DESCRIBE A HARD BASTARD

A hard bastard is someone, male or female, who can go through a real drama and come out the other side, dust themselves down, and carry on. Pure physical strength alone doesn't make you a hard bastard.

NAME A HARD BASTARD

In every street, in every town, there are hard bastards. People whose name you wouldn't know – you just pass them in the street. Most of them are unknown.

WHERE DO YOU SEE YOURSELF IN FIVE YEARS?

Writing best-sellers – just like you!

ANY REGRETS?

There are some people I would have liked to have dealt with when my mum was alive rather than now she's dead. Then she would have known that I dealt with them. That's the only regret I have.

I don't want to be seen as a tough guy. I don't want to hurt anybody. My little girl was at school and the teacher asked the kids to say what their mums and dads did for a living. My little girl said, 'My dad's a bumper.' So the teacher asked her what she meant. My daughter explained, 'He throws people out of clubs and beats them up.'

'Oh,' said the teacher. 'You mean a bouncer.'

But that's how my little girl saw me and I regret that. I don't want people to think of me like that. I want the kids I work with to think I'm a nice person and to respect me as someone who works hard. If I touch people's lives, I want to touch them in a positive way.

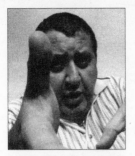

HARD BASTARD

Trevor - The Iron Man of Bolton

TREVOR - THE IRON MAN OF BOLTON

I waited in a service station on the outskirts of Coventry for the Iron Man of Bolton. Me and my boyfriend, Leo, were early. So we drank coffee, read the papers and waited and waited and waited ...

After a long while, we decided to go into the amusement arcade to while away the time. We had great fun on the brightly-lit machines; we raced each other with the Formula One racing cars, we shot enemies with laser guns and had a go on the 'electrocution' machine. (This involves holding hands and sharing an electric shock!)

We had a great laugh, such a great time that we hadn't noticed a large, stocky man watching us and shaking his head bemusedly. Yep ... it was the Iron Man of Bolton.

Usually when I go to meet a tough guy, I try to be cool, calm and in control. But, oops, not this time. Still, at least it broke the ice.

'Where,' I asked Trevor, 'did you get the name "Iron Man of Bolton"?'

He replied, 'I used to practise Ki, a sort of controlled breathing. Then I used to let people bite me and poke my eyes out. After that, I had to wear glasses so I had to pack it in. But the name came from my eye-poking days!'

I see ...

NAME: Trevor Roberts

DATE OF BIRTH: 19 January 1950

STAR SIGN: Capricorn

OCCUPATION: Security director

BACKGROUND

I'm from Bolton. I was 15 when I went into wrestling and I became a British wrestling champion twice. Then I started ju-jitsu and I won a British title and a European title. Then I went into a kind of judo which is very rough but it's a good crack. Now I've got my own association, my own style – Tatsu No Otoko Ryu. When I was a kid, it was either judo or wrestling – there was nothing else for you. I was always crying if I didn't win a prize!

My dad was the biggest influence in my life. If it wasn't for him, I don't think I'd be like I am. He wasn't a fighter, he was a nice fella. He was dead straight, worked all his life. Just like my mum.

LIFE OF CRIME
None really. I collect debts and things like that but I'm not what you'd call a villain.

DO YOU THINK THAT PRISON IS A DETERRENT?
Yes – I wouldn't want it.

DO YOU BELIEVE IN CAPITAL PUNISHMENT?
It depends on the crime. People hurting kids absolutely, yes.

WHAT DETERRED YOU FROM A LIFE OF CRIME?
I think I've always had a fun personality and I've always done what I wanted to do. On the door, people worked to my rules or they didn't work at all. I've lived my life that way. Maybe I'm just a lucky bugger.

HAVE YOU EVER BEEN STABBED/SHOT?
I've been shot at. I've taken a few knives off people. I've been cut when I've taken a blade off people. When someone's got a blade and you're surrounded by people and your life is on the line, you've got to react. I'm 19 stone ... my size and strength helps. But, initially, it's a question of sensing trouble – I've been at it so long, I can sense trouble a mile off.

SCARIEST MOMENT?

We had a massive gang fight at a pub outside Bolton. It was a Sunday night so we got a few doormen together. There were four of us – and lots of them. It might sound like I'm bragging but, honestly, there were quite a few of them. We were fighting for 45 minutes but it felt like for ever. It seemed that it would never stop. They were coming at us in waves. You'd fight someone off, then another one was on you. They'd come in the pub doors and then go back out, then come in again. It was a real set-to.

Tables went up in the air, glasses were smashed, bottles were thrown. It was like the Wild West ... and I'm no John Wayne.

SADDEST MOMENT

When my dad died last year. He had arthritis and hadn't walked for three years. When he stopped walking, everything started packing up on him.

WHAT RATTLES YOUR CAGE?

Cruelty to animals. I hate fox-hunting and, especially, dog-fighting. People who hurt defenceless animals are bastards, pure and simple. I used to be an inspector for the Staffordshire Bull Association. Some of the cruelty I witnessed would break your heart. Bastards – pure and simple.

HAVE YOU EVER REALLY LOVED ANYONE?

Yeah, my second wife. I thought the world of her – still do. We've split up but we're still best friends; she's still my best mate.

WHAT FRIGHTENS YOU?

Spiders. I hate them … nasty little hairy buggers.

DESCRIBE A HARD BASTARD

Being a hard bastard is all to do with mental attitude. If you've got the mental attitude and you're determined to do something – no matter what the odds – then you're going to do it.

I've been in bodyguarding situations where I've been sweating, but if you've got that mental attitude … being a hard bastard is definitely a state of mind. I mean, I've got a bloke working on the door now … he's 6ft 2in, a 23-stone body-builder, he's a skinhead with one of those pierced things through his eyebrow and you look at him and think, Jesus Christ! But he's as soft as shit. He's definitely not what he looks! Being a hard bastard is not a physical thing – it's definitely a state of mind.

NAME A HARD BASTARD

Frank Holt – he was an old wrestling champ of years ago. When I was first wrestling and I was 18 years old, he was the daddy of them all. He got away with murder. He broke iron bars – all sorts. He definitely wasn't the full shilling. He befriended me.

He went inside for a while and came out with nothing. He's got nothing now but he's a great old man.

WHERE DO YOU SEE YOURSELF IN FIVE YEARS?

We've got this company and if everything goes as it should in five years' time I'll be 57 and I'll be just about thinking of selling up and retiring. Then I want to go to Italy, travel around for nine months. The people are fanatastic, the food's fantastic, the weather's just right – the whole place is fabulous. I love it there. Great place.

ANY REGRETS?

Dozens, I suppose. But the biggest regret is the failure of my third marriage. You know what us Northerners are like – we know what we like and we like what we bloody well know.

HARD BASTARD

Brian
Thorogood

BRIAN THOROGOOD

Brian Thorogood is a robber. By the mid-Eighties he'd carried out 20 robberies, 16 of them using a sawn-off shotgun.

Now he looks like a 1960s gangster out of *Get Carter*. He's a really unassuming man – he doesn't look like an armed robber at all. In fact, he was one of the most fearsome armed robbers in London for many years. For a long time, the main men in the armed robber stakes were Mickey Calvey, Ronnie Cook and Brian Thorogood, and at one time or another they have all had one thing – or rather one love – in common: Linda Calvey.

Linda is the only real female gangster this country has ever had. Even the scriptwriters of *Prime Suspect* would find it hard to match the real-life drama of this East End girl with an insatiable appetite for excitement, a glamorous platinum blonde whose beauty has intoxicated so many men. The newspapers nicknamed her the Black Widow.

Linda is currently serving life for murder but we are in touch and through her I met Brian. Of course, I knew his name, I'd heard it in certain circles.

To understand Brian you have to understand the Black Widow story, the story of the woman he loved, the woman who accompanied him on his robberies.

The story begins in December 1978 on a busy Saturday afternoon outside a supermarket called Caters in Eltham in South London, where everyone had been busy Christmas shopping. It was just after closing time, dead on 6.00pm, when the armoured security van pulled up outside to collect the day's takings. It had been a good day and the cash bags were full – £10,000.

Just as the guards came out of the supermarket, a 3.5 Rover saloon screeched to a halt in front of the security van. Three robbers jumped out of the car, all armed with sawn-off shotguns. One of the robbers coshed a guard and grabbed a bag of money.

But the Flying Squad had been tipped off and were lying in wait. DS Michael Banks pulled out his .38 Smith and Wesson and shouted, 'Stop! We are armed police!'

The three robbers ignored them. Two jumped into the front of the car. DS Banks fired two shots at the car but missed. The third robber, 36-year-old Mickey Calvey, ran to the getaway car and tried to get in the back. With his gun in his hand and his arm outstretched, Banks yelled another warning, 'Stop, or I'll shoot!'

Mickey turned to face the policeman, his sawn-off

shotgun still in his hands. Banks fired two shots. Mickey Calvey slumped to the ground dead. Mickey was Linda's husband, the father of her children. She was devastated.

For Mickey Calvey, that was the end. But not for Linda.

After her husband's shooting, she became friends with another gangster, Ronnie Cook. Later, it was alleged that he had been one of the armed robbers who had got away with the £10,000 from the supermarket.

Cook helped Linda cope with her grief. He spent lavishly and soon the pair became inseparable. But it wasn't to last. Ronnie Cook was jailed in 1981, sentenced to 16 years for his part in yet another armed robbery.

Cook couldn't stand the thought of Linda being alone, so he arranged for a friend to help her.

Enter Brian Thorogood.

Brian, a former Royal Fusilier, was the next to fall under the spell of the Black Widow. He and Linda were soon involved in a passionate affair and eventually, after he had left his wife, he set up home with Linda in Hornchurch.

But the robberies continued. Brian was eventually jailed in 1985 for 21 years and this time he took Linda with him. She was found guilty of conspiracy to commit armed robbery and was sentenced to seven years, her first taste of prison.

With Brian in prison, Cook soon learned about his affair with Linda. Cook was furious and vowed to kill Brian if he ever caught up with him again. But Linda was different. Cook loved her and she convinced him that she was faithful, even having a tattoo done on her thigh with the words 'True love, Ronnie Cook'.

But all the time she was still writing to Brian.

Linda served four years of her seven-year stretch and by 1989 she was out. She continued to visit both Brian and Cook in their different prisons, until Cook became eligible for home leave from Maidstone Jail in November 1990.

Linda was fully aware of how violent Cook could become and when he discovered she had still been visiting Brian ... well ... together she and Brian hatched a plan.

He introduced her to a man called Danny Reece – 35-year-old Reece was serving 13 years at the Verne Prison in Portland, Dorset for violence. Linda went to meet Reece and it was there, while drinking tea with him in the visitor's hall under the noses of the prison guards that she asked Reece to shoot Ronnie Cook for a fee of £10,000.

Instantly he fell for her – and agreed to do the job.

Linda made all the arrangements. She would get Cook to the house in the late afternoon. Reece would be lying in wait.

So far – so bad. As Linda and Cook walked into the house, Reece burst in but when he came face to face with Ronnie Cook, he couldn't do it. He shot him in the elbow.

But Linda could.

She grabbed the gun from him and screamed, 'Kneel!' Then she pointed the gun and shot Ronnie Cook in the head.

Both Danny Reece and Linda Calvey were sentenced to life imprisonment in 1990.

Brian is out now.

Danny and Linda married in prison.

You see what I mean. It's quite a story, isn't it?

NAME: Brian Thorogood
DATE OF BIRTH: 22 December 1938
STAR SIGN: Capricorn
OCCUPATION: Armed Robber

BACKGROUND

I was brought up in the Mile End so I'm a Cockney, you'd better believe it. I come from a big family of six and I'm the youngest. They're all straight: I'm what you might call the black sheep.

LIFE OF CRIME

Out of the last 30 years, I've done about 21 years in prison. All for armed robbery, I'm afraid.

IS PRISON A DETERRENT?

Not for me it isn't, no. I don't know about kids today because so much of it all is drug-related but years ago, if you were a young offender, you got sent away and all that happened was you got educated. When you're younger, you want the money ... the older you get the more dangerous you get.

When you're out on armed robberies, of course, you think about getting shot, not about going to prison.

DO YOU BELIEVE IN CAPITAL PUNISHMENT?

Yes, in certain cases. Bad cases involving women and children. But not for armed robbers!

WHAT WOULD HAVE DETERRED YOU FROM A LIFE OF CRIME?

Winning the pools. It's all about money. When I was with Linda for that three or four years, everything I touched turned to gold.

HAVE YOU EVER BEEN STABBED/SHOT?

Yes, stabbed and shot. Twice stabbed and once shot – that time I was told later I had about 20 minutes to live but I woke up, thank God.

SCARIEST MOMENT?

Falling in love – with a certain person.

SADDEST MOMENT?

What's happened to Linda, that makes me sad … she doesn't deserve it … All those things I've done in my life, all the time I've spent inside, well, that's one thing, I've got no regrets. But Linda getting life and what happened to her before that … that is so sad. What's happened to that poor girl is wrong.

WHAT RATTLES YOUR CAGE?

Not much, but one or two really do rattle me. I try to live by a certain set of principles. One is that if I give my word to someone, I keep it, it matters. I hate it when other people break their word. And people being late. That really pisses me off.

HAVE YOU EVER REALLY LOVED ANYONE?

Linda Calvey. I still love her, even though she's now married to Danny Reece.

WHAT FRIGHTENS YOU?

No comment.

DESCRIBE A HARD BASTARD

A hard bastard is a stupid bastard. I'd rather be a friend. There is a difference between a hard bastard and an evil bastard.

NAME A HARD BASTARD

No comment.

WHERE DO YOU SEE YOURSELF IN FIVE YEARS?

God knows.

ANY REGRETS?

None I want to talk about.

HARD BASTARD

Marco

MARCO

Marco is a Hell's Angel – and that means a lot. He runs a pub – named Goodfellows after the gangster film – and you know you've got the right place because Marco's Harley Davidson is parked right outside and inside his Hell's Angels of England jacket, with colours, is lying on a table.

I did a bit of research about the Hell's Angels before I met Marco because I know little about them and, like a lot of other people I suppose, I have this picture in my head of men with big beards, long, grubby hair, perhaps holding a bottle of Jack Daniels in one hand and, of course, wearing the well-worn leather jacket with skull and crossbones.

Well, I was right about the jacket. But as for my idea of bikers surrounded by snakes and naked ladies – forget it!

The Hell's Angels live by a code of honour and silence.

I knew Marco wouldn't let me into too many secrets, so I had to ask around. What I found out was astonishing – the Hell's Angels are the fastest-growing, criminal (some would say) organisation in the world.

They earn money – big money. The organisation is made up of different clubs all over the world. America is big on Hell's Angels but Europe is rapidly becoming big, too. Yet here, in the UK, I was told there are only about 12 genuine Hell's Angels clubs with between 20 members to just five or six in each – that's just 200 true Hell's Angels. And, at the moment, there are a lot of 'wars', fierce rivalries in which people are actually getting killed.

So, there aren't many genuine Hell's Angels – although there are obviously a lot of wannabes – because getting into what is really a brotherhood is no easy matter. Being a Hell's Angel is a total lifestyle. There are a lot of parties but a lot of jealousies, too, especially when a new member comes in and wants to make a reputation for himself.

To become a member of the club, first you have got to convince the other members about who you are, about your honesty and integrity because, to its members and to others, it is a very prestigious club. It takes a lot to get in but not much to be thrown out – lying is one thing that will get you out real quick – and a good beating to go with it. If you are caught thieving from another member, it will cost you everything: it will ruin your life.

To get in, someone usually shows an interest by simply turning up to drink wherever the Angels are drinking. There's a 'hanging around' period of about a year. Then there's a year of what the Angels call 'prospecting', when

Trevor – The Iron Man of Bolton

Brian Thorogood

Marco

Kalvinder Dhesi

Lou Yates

Duchy Peter

Dominic

Manchester Tony

you get Hell's Angels on the back of your jacket, the Death's head and the name of your club. Next you might become a sergeant, making sure everyone is 'taken care of' – whatever that means – and you have to prove your worth and worthiness. If you're up to it and if you get a 100 per cent 'yes' vote from your club, you get in.

And once you're in, you're accepted by Hell's Angels all over the world. Hell's Angels do business in Africa, America, Australia and, wherever they travel, they never have to take cash – apparently, you just get off a plane, ring a contact and they will fix you up with accommodation, money and, of course, transport!

It all sounded very impressive, albeit in a bit of a scary way. So driving over to Marco's pub, I felt a bit apprehensive. Getting an interview with this genuine Hell's Angel for this book had been hard – harder than getting Johnny Adair, the terrorist; harder than getting the gangsters; harder than getting the Triads.

The reason is simple – they all stick together. They have to go in front of a 'board' and have every other member's seal of approval before they agree to talk to you, or they're not allowed to talk to you.

In the event the pub turned out to be smashing – just a normal, very nice pub. Marco was intelligent, charming, witty, and quite flattering in the things he said to me. The first thing I noticed when we met was his jewellery – lots of it and lots of Death's heads – closely followed by his piercing blue eyes which momentarily met mine. There was no grubby long hair, no beard – he was strikingly neat and tidy – and the Jack Daniels was behind the bar.

But his neatness was offset by an unmistakable whiff of raw power. You can see in his eyes if he likes you ... But if he doesn't ...

NAME: Marco
DATE OF BIRTH: 7 September 1952
STAR SIGN: Virgo
OCCUPATION: Licensee and Hell's Angel

BACKGROUND

I'm half-Italian. I was brought up in East London – Peckham, Barking, Whitechapel. When I worked in a club, they called me a Cockney Wop.

It wasn't what you'd call a normal childhood I suppose – I was brought up in children's homes, then Borstal, then prison. There were seven of us in my family – four sisters and three brothers. I was second down, second eldest.

LIFE OF CRIME

A little bit. I've been in prison for affray, armed robbery – kid's stuff. I've done four years all told.

IS PRISON A DETERRENT?

No. You're the only deterrent, it's up to you – prison is just something you get on top. Age doesn't deter you either. I think the older you get, the wilder you should get. You don't want to end up in a hospice somewhere. Why do you want to calm down as you get older? If you calm down, you die.

DO YOU BELIEVE IN CAPITAL PUNISHMENT?
No. I don't think it deters anyone from anything. If you're going to kill someone, you're going to kill them. You're not going to sit there thinking about it, about what's going to happen to you.

WHAT WOULD HAVE DETERRED YOU FROM A LIFE OF CRIME?
I haven't had a life of crime – but nothing would deter you. I believe you've got to live your life the way you want to live it and don't let anything deter you from that because otherwise you spend your life regretting it.

HAVE YOU EVER BEEN STABBED/SHOT?
Neither. I've been shot at – but never shot.

SCARIEST MOMENT?
I think going out with a girl for the first time was the scariest.

SADDEST MOMENT?
Getting dumped by the girl!

WHAT RATTLES YOUR CAGE?
Bullshit pisses me off. People who try to impress you,

name droppers, all that. People who try to get round you, who fake friendship.

HAVE YOU EVER REALLY LOVED ANYONE?

Yes. Once. I believe you only ever really love once. I don't think you know when you're in love – you only know it when you've lost it. But it's definitely true that it's better to have loved and lost than never to have loved at all.

WHAT FRIGHTENS YOU?

Living too long. Living too long and not being capable of doing things for yourself. I'd hate to have to be looked after, walking around with a Zimmer frame, walking up the road talking to yourself and swearing at people, all that kind of thing.

DESCRIBE A HARD BASTARD

A Smith and Wesson.

NAME A HARD BASTARD

A Glock.

WHERE DO YOU SEE YOURSELF IN FIVE YEARS?

Exactly what I'm doing now. Being a Hell's Angel. I enjoy my life. Being a Hell's Angel is being a total, honest, genuine person to another brother, a club member. There's nothing you wouldn't do for that person, you'd go to jail for that person, you'd die for that person if you had to.

To me, if you've got a friend, you'd do anything for that friend and you expect that back. There's no excuses.

What we've got is, I think, what a lot of people want – they want to know that if something happens to them, their family would be looked after not just for a while but for years if necessary. To become a Hell's Angel you have to be over 21, be a male, have a Harley Davidson and have it in your heart to become a Hell's Angel and live by the code. It takes about two or three years. You only wear colours when you become a full member.

I've been a Hell's Angel since I was 18 – they've changed the age now to 21 – but I joined when I was 18. The Hell's Angels have conquered more countries than any other force in history. There are Hell's Angels everywhere. We're not all the same, we're all individuals. We don't all like rock music. But we've all got one thing in common – we all want to keep our independence. We're a democracy. If anything has to be decided, the majority rules. If you want to do something – like this interview – you go to a meeting. It's discussed and a vote is taken and then you abide by that.

If the vote had gone that I shouldn't talk to you for this book I would have abided by that.

ANY REGRETS?

No. I'd do it all again.

HARD BASTARD

Kalvinder Dhesi

KALVJNDER DHESJ

On his right shoulder Kalvinder – or Kal as everyone knows him – has a fearsome tattoo of two crossed swords. This marks the fact that he is a Sikh warrior.

Kal is a big, powerful, Asian man and he's proud to be Asian. He's also proud to be a Sikh. And he's also one hard bastard.

Kal is well-known within Asian communities. Inevitably, the Asian community has its own clubs, its own gangs and its own tough guys to control those clubs. Kal is a troubleshooter for a lot of Asian clubs in the south-east.

Being Asian, Kal has had to put up with his share of racism. His smashing girlfriend, the mother of his children, is white so she gets it, too.

I loathe racism – my mother is half-cast so I grew up

witnessing racial hatred and I understood what they were talking about. But I was shocked when she talked to me. She told me that older Asians had spat at her and Kal in their own home town when their youngest was a baby.

'The baby was crying so Kal picked him up and people kept looking at us,' she said. 'Because the baby is quite light-skinned, they couldn't imagine what Kal was doing picking up this baby. Most people are OK, but I do think the older generation have a problem with mixed-race relationships and families.

'All Kal's friends have been brilliant – they've never looked at us differently, but when my first baby was very young I do remember someone looking in the pram and saying, "Look at that black baby there." I've never forgotten that and I never will.'

Kal and his family live in a huge, flash house with electric gates and a Mercedes in the drive on the outskirts of Kent. He is not, definitely not, the stereotype of what people expect an Asian businessman to be. He doesn't run a corner shop for a start!

He was nervous when he met me and a little bit suspicious. Everything about him was big – the house, the car, even his hands, and he shook mine with a vice-like grip.

But he was very polite and very softly spoken. He had eyes like crushed black velvet … an interesting man, I think, and, maybe, a dangerous one.

NAME: Kal
DATE OF BIRTH: 24 July 1965
STAR SIGN: Leo
OCCUPATION: Door supervisor in Rochester

BACKGROUND

I've worked on doors for the last 12 years. It wasn't something I set out to do but I got the job because of my reputation; it came along, I took it and 12 years later I'm still doing it.

I was born in Plumstead. My mum and dad were from India originally. I'm the second of three brothers. We're three very different characters. I suppose I'm what you might call the black sheep of the family. I'm divorced and I've got four kids – two from my last marriage and two from a previous relationship. If any of my kids ever wanted to do door work, I'd have a serious talk with them, a very serious talk.

LIFE OF CRIME

I've been in prison but it was a short sentence – 28 days. I was done for possession of firearms, cannabis and stolen goods. It was all around the time of the firearms amnesty in the late Eighties. I had a shotgun and didn't hand it in and someone grassed on me.

IS PRISON A DETERRENT?

No. Inside you meet other inmates who are into other things, you learn things. Basically it's an education for criminals.

DO YOU BELIEVE IN CAPITAL PUNISHMENT?

Yes, for child molesters and paedophiles. Personally, I think they should be tortured first; they should go through mental and physical hell. Straightforward capital punishment is too easy for them.

WHAT WOULD HAVE DETERRED YOU FROM A LIFE OF CRIME?

Nothing.

HAVE YOU EVER BEEN STABBED/SHOT?

No.

SCARIEST MOMENT?

I don't know. I can't think of any scary moments.

SADDEST MOMENT?

When me mum and me nan passed away. My mum passed away four years ago and my nan just recently.

WHAT RATTLES YOUR CAGE?

Racism. Racist abuse. I did used to get a lot of it when I first started on the door at Rochester after I'd turned people away, and endured a lot of comments. I used to snap but I've accepted it now. I ignore it. But then sometimes I can snap just like that because I don't see why you should get treated like that because of your colour.

If I turn someone away from the door, it isn't because of their colour, there's always a valid reason. Other doormen – white doormen – don't get that abuse so why should I? I have been arrested a few times when I've retaliated. When I'm not working I get it, too, and – especially if I'm with the kids – I don't retaliate. I just ignore it and walk on.

I do think things have improved in Britain since the early Eighties. It's better now than it used to be. People are more tolerant. And I don't think it depends on whether you live North or South. It all depends on what the situation is like where you are – unemployment, housing, things like that. I've worked the door on Asian clubs and sometimes I've had more trouble there than in mixed clubs! Then there's the problems of caste, religion ... all that. But here in Rochester I get respect from Asian people and no trouble from local people and if they've got any grief, I'll try and sort it out.

HAVE YOU EVER REALLY LOVED ANYONE?
Yes. My girlfriend.

WHAT FRIGHTENS YOU?
Anything to do with my kids being hurt. That frightens me. I was with my son a few years ago in the park and he fell into a pool. I grabbed his arm and he was OK but I was in a state, I was sweating all day. I felt so utterly helpless, sick.

DESCRIBE A HARD BASTARD

Someone who is fair and firm and who can deal with complications without going out and getting guns. Someone who can assess a situation and deal with it nicely, verbally, always firm and fair. If it comes to it – then fair enough. But a hard bastard can make someone walk away from a fight. There's nothing wrong with swallowing your pride and walking away from a fight that's unnecessary.

NAME A HARD BASTARD

Roy Shaw.

WHERE DO YOU SEE YOURSELF IN FIVE YEARS?

I haven't thought about it. Maybe still doing the door – but who knows?

ANY REGRETS?

None whatsoever.

HARD BASTARD

Lou Yates

LOU YATES

Ferrets, whippets, flat caps and coal ... and some nasty bastards.

That's it. I know they're clichés, but that's about all I know about north of the border – north of the border being anywhere past the Watford Gap! Get me north of Watford and I'm lost!

But I wanted to include some Northern hard bastards in this book, so I started ringing around and asking well-known tough guys. There's Charlie Seiga, of course. And quite a few others. But one name kept cropping up time and time again – 'Wild Thing'.

'Wild Thing?' I kept asking.

'Wild Thing – you know, Lou Yates.'

I didn't, but I soon found out. Some said he was the best doorman, not just up North, but in London, too.

Nah, I thought, I can't believe that.

Others said he was a champion bare-knuckle fighter in the Seventies – even going up against the likes of Pretty Boy Shaw.

Nah, didn't believe that either.

The two things everyone agreed on was his size – he's as big as a semi-detached – and his jolly sense of humour.

Well, I just had to track this happy monster down and find out for myself. It took two days of ringing around and – Bingo! – I was on my way to a meeting. And from the moment we met, Wild Thing and I got on like a house on fire.

It didn't matter how many ferret or whippet snipes I made to Lou, he'd just throw back his head and laugh. Then he'd come back with a few jipes about nancy Southerners – quite right, too!

And that's how it's been every time we talk – and we talk often, because Lou does love a chat. When he rings, I know I'm going to be on the phone for an hour, a good hour, not talking about anything in particular, just laughing and listening to Lou laughing raucously.

Lou wants to write about his life. If he does, one thing is for sure; there will be plenty of words, plenty of laughs, thoughts, happiness – and plenty of sadness too.

Lou has been through it all and come out laughing, and that's no bad thing. Perhaps we can all learn a thing or two from Lou and from his experiences. I know I have – ferrets bite!

NAME: Lou Yates
DATE OF BIRTH: 3rd June 1951
STAR SIGN: Leo
OCCUPATION: Doorman and bare-
knuckle fighter

BACKGROUND

I was brought up in Lancashire – we were just a normal, average family. I've got one brother and two sisters – I don't have anything to do with them now. I was a little bastard when I was growing up. I wouldn't say I found trouble or trouble found me – it was 50-50.

I think I've always fought because my mother used to say to me, 'Why do you always talk with your fists?' I used to say to my mother, 'The reason I talk with my fists is that every bastard understands it.' I'm the same now. It's a universal language, isn't it?

I was 18 when I started working the door. I'd been kicked out – not literally – from this club, the best one in town. Even the Beatles played there once in the early days. At Christmas I went back to go in again. I got called over and I thought, Oh God, they're going to kick me out again.

Instead, the owner said, 'Do you want to work over Christmas? Work with us. We need some extra men. If you're interested, see the manager in the office.'

And that was that. That's how I started. I was training hard, I never used to drink but I trained a lot. Train, train, train all the time. But the first night on the door, a couple of the bouncers took me up the road to a pub for a drink in the early evening before the club opened. I had a couple of scotches and I was gone, because I never used to drink. I learned a lot very quickly! It was a great challenge.

People knew I was a boxer – my name had been in the papers – and there were these 30-year-olds I had to take care of. I was only a lad. It was a challenge all right and one I relished. It set the pattern for my adult life.

LIFE OF CRIME

Nothing heavy. I've never been in prison. I've been very, very lucky. I have been arrested lots of times – always violence, and always innocent, of course!

DO YOU THINK PRISON IS A DETERRENT?

To a degree – but not for everyone, no. A lot of people just come out and do it again. Well, you learn more in there, don't you? You meet mates in there and, when you come out, it just snowballs.

DO YOU BELIEVE IN CAPITAL PUNISHMENT?

I don't know. When I was a child, when I was younger, my uncle was birched. When he died of lung cancer, when he was 60 or whatever, he still had those marks on his back. He was only a kid. That was all wrong. It didn't do anything to change things. So capital punishment, I really don't know …

WHAT WOULD HAVE DETERRED YOU FROM A LIFE OF CRIME?

I haven't had a life of crime as such, but if I'd have lived in London I would have been very involved in it, definitely. The excitement of it. But where I came from, there wasn't that much, not like the people down South. I was a Northern bastard!

HAVE YOU EVER BEEN STABBED/SHOT?

I've been stabbed twice. Once in the back and once in the arm – both times working the doors. The strange thing about being stabbed is, at the time, you don't know at all, you don't feel it right then – you feel it afterwards, you feel the wetness of the blood.

When I was stabbed, I didn't know at all. I finished work in Barking – I'd had to fight off about 15 roughnecks that night. It was one of those nights. When I finished work, I used to call into a pub on my way home and my friend who ran it used to pay me to help him close up and get rid of the people who wouldn't leave. I went in there after I'd been stabbed and I didn't even realise I'd been stabbed. I met my wife in there and I took my jacket off and she said, 'You've got blood all over your back.' They looked and there was a wound at the base of the spine about an inch-and-a-half deep.

I looked in a mirror and the blood was just pumping out. The medics said if it had been an inch further over, I'd probably have been paralysed. But it wasn't. I was OK.

Have I been shot at? Oh yes, more than once. Of course more than once! You work the doors, you expect it. But there have been so many incidents over the years, I forget them.

SCARIEST MOMENT?

To be honest, no bullshitting, I don't really get frightened about things. I remember one man pulling a shooter on me when I was on the door and saying, 'You're going to die, you bastard.' I said, 'Well, go on then, fucking kill me. Go on, shoot me.'

I said it three times. I knew then that he wasn't going to shoot me. He was a young lad, he'd been in the Army in Northern Ireland so he knew what he was doing. I watched him pull the gun and load the magazine. But he didn't want to shoot me, not really. I told him just to put the gun in his pocket. I started to walk towards him saying, 'You can frighten people with that. Just put it in your pocket and go.'

He said, 'You're not going to try anything, are you?'

I said, 'No.' In fact, I just wanted to get close to him. In a flash, I saw my chance, grabbed hold of him, got the gun out of his pocket and hit him over the head with it. He went down immediately. I took him around the corner and dumped him there. The bloke from the kebab shop called the Old Bill and about 12 of them arrived with guns.

But it was all sorted out. I explained what had happened and said I didn't want him nicked. The lad now calls me a mate. But that was a bit scary at the time.

SADDEST MOMENT?

When my mum and dad died. My dad died of heart

problems in his seventies and I think Mum died in sympathy a while later. I think she wished herself to death after Dad died. After he went that's all she talked about – 'I want to die to be with Dad.'

WHAT RATTLES YOUR CAGE?
Mouthy bastards, loud people.

HAVE YOU EVER REALLY LOVED ANYONE?
My kids. My mum, although I used to get beatings from her. My dad used to do it on instructions from my mother. I loved her but she had a terrible, terrible temper.

WHAT FRIGHTENS YOU?
Not violence, violence doesn't frighten me at all, because I've never lost a street fight since I left school. All the clubs I've worked – I've never come unstuck. I think now, at my age, I think falling in love with someone would frighten me.

DESCRIBE A HARD BASTARD
A hard bastard has got to be hard physically and hard mentally. A real hard bastard has got to be both.

NAME A HARD BASTARD
Roy Shaw.

WHERE DO YOU SEE YOURSELF IN FIVE YEARS?
Prison, maybe.

There are people who have betrayed me and I wake up

morning after morning thinking I might just do them all – and I just might.

ANY REGRETS?

Yes. I regret never going to America when I was boxing. My life would have been very different then. I would have done well in America when I was younger if I hadn't got married early. All that.

HARD BASTARD

Duchy Peter

DUCHY PETER

Duchy wears extraordinary gold jewellery – one piece is a man's gold tooth, a molar on a chain. He ripped it out of a geezer's mouth after a fight.

Un-fucking-believable – that's the only word I can think of to describe Duchy. He is just that.

I'd heard of this man who was a mean mother****** who had been nicked for this and that, who'd worked the doors – apparently, he was a musician, bouncer, fighter, tough guy, black, charismatic, great talker … and as if that wasn't enough, he was a victim of thalidomide as a child, and has no legs.

Like I said, un-fucking-believable! It's easy to be patronising about disabled people and, I must admit, when I first went to see Duchy, all the stereotypes ran through my mind. I hadn't been in his flat long before I realised that *I* was the disabled person – I couldn't do half the things that Duchy does and I've got both my pins.

Here is a man who has been dealt a poxy hand in life. But he has jumped up, grabbed life by the neck, shook the living daylights out of it and then some. Duchy is an inspiration. I'm not just saying that because of his disability but because of the way he has handled – and continues to handle – what's been thrown at him; he has no legs, he has a disabled sister, he had a miserable childhood, he was put into care, he's been in prison, and his wife left him to bring up their children on his own. Shall I go on?

That's enough to bring anyone to their knees (sorry, Duchy!)

He's just taken on a new door job in south-east London. He's incredibly fit, weightlifts, works out, plays golf, and he's a karate black belt.

He's also a very interesting, if introspective, man.

I think when God has to dish out the crappy things in his medical box, he dishes it out to people who he knows are strong enough to cope. Duchy is one of those. I'm glad I met him.

NAME: Duchy Peter
DATE OF BIRTH: 26 September 1963
STAR SIGN: Libra
OCCUPATION: Musician-cum-bouncer

BACKGROUND

I was born in Lewisham, South London. I was brought up in Limehouse and went to a school for the physically disabled, which I shouldn't have done because I was the only able-bodied person there. I was fostered from an early age – I didn't go back to my parents until later on.

It wasn't an easy upbringing; it was hard, complicated. I went from children's home to children's home. Then I got totally uncontrollable and got packed off to East London where I learned to be naughty!

I haven't always been a fighter. I used to be a real coward but then I got really fed up with getting hit. I suddenly realised that if you barked at the world, it jumped – you know what I mean. Think about it. If the world barks at you, you jump, don't you? If you bark back, it makes life a little bit easier.

Perhaps at heart I was always a fighter because you've got to be a fighter to live with the disability I've got and be able to deal with it. Now I've come to the conclusion that I'm always going to be fighting, whether it's British Telecom or the Council or the big old geezer up the road who parks his van on the corner so I can't get my wheelchair past. I'm always going to be a fighter but I have to be. That's my life now and I've accepted that. To live with this disability day to day you must be a fighter. I've obviously thought a lot about my disability, God, all that. I do agree that God gives disabilities to strong people.

I also believe that he gives you this disability to slow you down a bit because I don't know what I would have been like without this disability. I've had my friends say that to me – I would have been a horrible this or that! As it is, I like the person I am, I really do.

There was a time when I didn't like myself when the old skulduggery slipped in, but I can look back. I did a bit of bird and I think it was when I was going in front of my parole board and they read out my record and I shivered and I thought, Well, I'll never get parole. Then they read the new report and I thought I wasn't a nice person at all, not at all. I had thought I was a nice person, but I wasn't. That changed me, but I think I've still got to do a little bit of learning now.

LIFE OF CRIME

The skulduggery started when I was 16. A lot of it was to do with the institutions I was in. My sister is mentally handicapped – she couldn't get out. But I could; I got out with my mates and I thought, Well, if *they're* up to skulduggery, then *I'm* up to skulduggery, too. You wouldn't believe the amount of times I got nicked and allowed myself to be carried home!

Since then I've done enough bird to know I don't want to go inside again. It was never violence as such – I'm a disciplined martial artist. I was done for allowing myself to be carrying offensive weapons.

IS PRISON A DETERRENT?

If you're the norm – yes. If you're a person with a bit of life, ambition and substance – yes it is. But if you're not, no it isn't.

There are loads of people who get up in the morning, whack something up the nose, drink down the pub 24 hours a day, go and nick this or that – for them, no. If you've got some substance in your life, you feel prison. If you haven't got a home you're not too bothered where you sleep, are you? I've got substance in my life now. If I'm in prison, I miss my kid, I miss being at home, I miss being with my mates down the pub.

I think the facilities in prison for the disabled are terrible now – I did my bird quite easy – but you wouldn't now. The prison service can't cope with disabled people.

DO YOU BELIEVE IN CAPITAL PUNISHMENT?

Yes, definitely, I do. People who sexually assault and hurt kids. Don't torture them – I'm not into the torture game, that makes us as bad as them. But, certainly, string them up. I honestly believe that if these people knew they would be killed if they hurt or sexually assaulted a child, if they knew they'd be strung up, they wouldn't do it.

WHAT WOULD HAVE DETERRED YOU FROM A LIFE OF CRIME?

Having a proper job. Being respected in the community. It didn't work out like that. If you pick a fight with me, you deserve to get beaten up because you're the kind of person who would take £5 off my mum in the street.

HAVE YOU EVER BEEN STABBED/SHOT?

I've never been shot, but I've been stabbed in the hand.

SCARIEST MOMENT?

I was once on a boat with my family in the Caribbean. It was three in the morning and I had a nightmare. I suddenly woke up and for some reason I thought my mum was dead. I woke everyone else up and said, 'Get up, up, we're going back to Britain now. NOW!' It was a strange gut feeling, really strong, very scary.

SADDEST MOMENT?

Losing my child, my baby. He was five months old and called DJ – Duch Junior. That day was the worst of my life. The pain was so bad it was physical.

WHAT RATTLES YOUR CAGE?

I can't abide stupidness – stupid rules – don't do this, don't do that …

HAVE YOU EVER REALLY LOVED ANYONE?

Leave it out – why do you think I'm on my Jack Jones? I could never love anyone else, can't imagine myself shacked up with any other woman, not the sort of man I am. Love and hate are so close together – if that was love, why do I feel like this now?

I feel so full of hate and bitterness. So how can I say I love. Love is love; love means loving someone endlessly, no matter what they do.

WHAT FRIGHTENS YOU?

My father was a vicar. He's now retired. Only him.

DESCRIBE A HARD BASTARD
Someone who can take it, take it, take it!

NAME A HARD BASTARD
My mum.

WHERE DO YOU SEE YOURSELF IN FIVE YEARS?
Sitting on a yacht in Miami, listening to music and contemplating my next film deal!

ANY REGRETS?
Not really – you come in with nothing, you go out with nothing. Well, maybe, I should have listened to my elders when I was young. Then, perhaps, I wouldn't have had such a hard time growing up.

HARD BASTARD

Dominic

DOMJNJC

The Milky Bar Kid is strong and tough ... and only the best is good enough. Yep ... that just about sums up Dominic.

Dominic is a big, strong man even if his nickname is The Milky Bar Kid. He's no nerdy geek with glasses. Dominic is a boxer, a heavyweight, a no-messing weight, a knock-out weight.

Normally, I wouldn't include a boxer in my book, although they are all tough guys and disciplined. Boxing is a sport. Mind you, I think boxing and skulduggery have always gone hand in hand to a certain extent ... in certain circles. Many of the villains I've known or been involved with have been involved with boxing to some degree. It's a way of releasing aggression, and many villains are aggressive. To be honest, many of them love a tear-up and better in the ring than in the street. And if you're going to box, then you want to do it well.

Dominic does it well ... he is a hard bastard.

> **NAME:** Dominic. Why do you want to know?
> Can I call my solicitor?
>
> **DATE OF BIRTH:** 28 July 1970
>
> **STAR SIGN:** Leo
>
> **OCCUPATION:** I'm a professional
> fighter and that's it – honest!

BACKGROUND

I was born in Bethnal Green. I was brought up in Essex, like in Woodford. It was just a normal upbringing, you know what I mean; we didn't have much, but it was normal. I can't say it was bad – I've got a brother and, we had our mum and dad who looked after us.

I suppose I was a bit of an animal from the beginning – I mean, I got expelled from junior school. But once I went to senior school it was different. I was a little fish in a big pond, then. I left school at 15, worked as a car-sprayer, got good money, really good money, then I got fed up with working. So I started doing the doors at 18 and then I worked all over the place. I worked at The Astoria, The Venue, Dingwalls ... The thing was, even at 18, I was always game. Even though I had curly hair and glasses – they used to call me The Milky Bar Kid – I was always game. I wouldn't take shit off anyone. I worked with a gang of lorry drivers and once they saw me in a pair of shorts and they said, 'Look, it's Milky!' I didn't have bandy legs but I was very white and the name stuck. But it's actually served me well – it's a comical name people remember. It's done well for me in boxing, too, because kids coming into the game now all like to call themselves Killer or Terminator. I laugh my head off when I'm fighting because they hear that comical name but I'm a born fighter; fighters aren't made they're born. I think I've wanted to fight since I was born.

I suppose I started seriously when I was 20 or 21, but I was always rucking before that. I was involved in street fighting before that but, basically, I'm a boxer – and a very good boxer at that. If I could combine everything I've got and if I could listen to my trainer – and he's known me for 12 years now – he says if I can just listen, I'll beat anyone. I enjoy fighting – I always have and always will.

IS PRISON A DETERRENT?

Yes and no, I suppose. You go inside these days and you come out with more knowledge and more connections than you ever had before. Then again, some people go in and come out different people than they ever were before. I do think that going into prison kills your soul – I'd never want to go away if I could help it. I've always wanted to be a free bird.

The life I've got at the moment is very good – I work hard. Don't get me wrong, because there's the boxing, but the other work I do, like the debt-collecting, it's a hard game because you're always walking in everyone else's shit. It isn't like saying to someone, 'Give me the fucking money' – it's hard. Like me and this other fella, we went to this big Turkish drinking den and there's only us two there and there must have been 20 geezers there – I don't carry anything with me because I don't need anything.

Once inside, they took us to the cellar and we talked and they're all there with cues and everything, and you think you just don't need the aggro, but you've got to do it anyway. Without going into too much detail, we walked out with the dough.

But there really are days when you wake up and think, I don't want to go to work today. I really don't want to do that today. But you've got to – that's where you get your money. We're not horrible people. We'd much rather sit down and work it out.

We're doing a debt at the moment – an old fella – you can't get blood out of a stone. But he still owes money. It's very frustrating, but first you talk. You know when someone's having you on and when someone's telling the truth. It's easy – they owe the money, we want it back.

Sometimes, it's not only the money, it's the principle that matters. We have a 98 per cent success rate – we haven't had to touch anyone really.

DO YOU BELIEVE IN CAPITAL PUNISHMENT?

For nonces, yes, definitely. If I had kids and someone hurt them, I'd hunt them down and I'd do bird for it. Someone fucks about with your kids, you'd do them, wouldn't you? You wouldn't even think about it.

WHAT DETERRED YOU FROM A LIFE OF CRIME?

Looking at other people – and what's happened to them as a result.

HAVE YOU EVER BEEN STABBED/SHOT?

I got a little nick once – that was the first night I worked at the Astoria. I've been threatened a few times but I think if they threaten you they aren't going to do it. But the life we lead, you've got to expect it, haven't you?

SCARIEST MOMENT?

Upsetting my mum I think. My mum's an outlaw – I'd rather fight Tyson any day!

SADDEST MOMENT?

Women make for the saddest moments. Most men say they're as hard as nails, but when it comes to women – I wear my heart on my sleeve which, I suppose, makes me the person I am but it also means I've been hurt by women.

WHAT RATTLES YOUR CAGE?

Rudeness. I do like manners in people. If you're on the door and people don't say, 'Thank you', that gives me the fucking hump, that does. If you open the door for someone these days, you try and be nice to them, you say, 'Hello' and 'How are you?' and they think you're mad! All I want is to be happy – I suppose I am a happy-go-lucky person. You expect a thank you. When you don't get one, that aggravates me.

HAVE YOU EVER REALLY LOVED ANYONE?

Yes. I loved and she done me like a kipper – and that really hurt. So for the last four years or so it's been hard for people to employ me because they know I'll take it as far as it can go. Why not? I'm on my own, I'm a single man. I have nothing to lose.

WHAT FRIGHTENS YOU?

Spiders.

DESCRIBE A HARD BASTARD

Someone who is willing to stand up for what he believes in. Some people out there are physically hard but not mentally – as soon as you get into their nuts, they're in trouble. A hard bastard will do anything for what he believes in – his family, his friends. My loyalty is to my friends; I'd do anything for my friends and they know that.

NAME A HARD BASTARD

One Mr Dark. I don't hero-worship him but he's as close to family as I'm going to get and the toughest man I've ever met.

WHERE DO YOU SEE YOURSELF IN FIVE YEARS?

Hopefully not in prison – hopefully settled with a wife and kids, people I can trust. Because there's one thing I know – there's too many dogs out there. There seems to be so little trust out there nowadays.

ANY REGRETS?

No. Whatever I've done I'd stand up for every day of the week. Some things I've done wrong and I think, I've been a bit lucky there. But then, the important things, the ones that matter, if I've done wrong I've always held my hands up to it. So no regrets.

HARD BASTARD

Manchester Tony

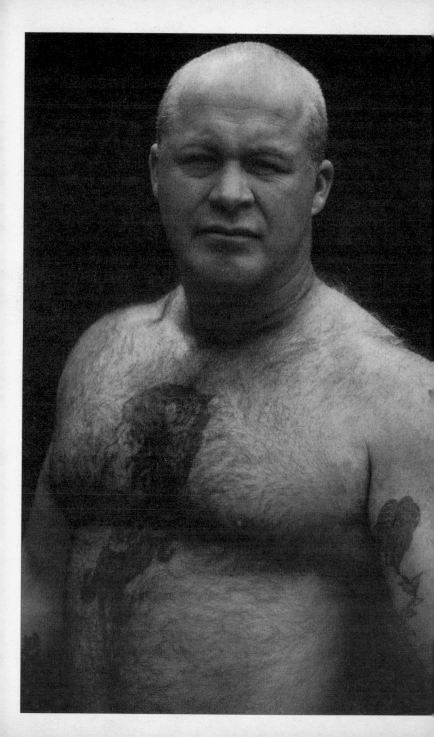

MANCHESTER TONY

Manchester Tony loves his dogs, his British bulldogs. And you know what they say about owners growing to look like their dogs – or is it vice versa? I'm sorry, Tony, but you do look strikingly similar and I mean that in the nicest possible way!

I drove to a new housing estate in the depths of the Garden of England – Kent – to meet Manchester Tony. I know – odd! I sat on his plush leather sofa and a brand-new Merc was parked in the drive. Tony handed me a drink in a crystal flute while he shooed his beloved dogs out for a wee.

He was wearing a dark-blue suit which looked like Armani (although I was too embarrassed to ask), he grinned a huge grin and rubbed his hands. 'Well, whatya want to know?'

He told me about his army days ... and about his dogs. He told me about his time inside ... and his dogs. He told me about Manchester ... and his dogs. I didn't mind. I'm a dog lover, too. So I told him about my two dogs ... and my parrot.

Then we got on to the subject of door work – and fighting. Gone was the beaming smile and the niceties. Out the window with the fluted crystal and even his beloved dogs were given a quick shufty up the bollocks, and the kitchen door slammed behind them.

Tony came alive and I saw the real Manchester Tony. Now it was my turn to grin and rub my hands, now we were talking ...

NAME: Manchester Tony

DATE OF BIRTH: 4 March 1962

STAR SIGN: Pisces

OCCUPATION: Gym owner and doorman

BACKGROUND

I'm originally from Manchester – obviously – but I came down to London when I was in the Army. I wasn't in for long – went in at 16, came out at 18. I ended up marrying a girl down here in Woolwich so I stayed. I didn't want to go back to Manchester – there was a bit of a family situation; they didn't like me up there. Manchester is much more segregated than London; people keep to their own areas – it's all to do with race. I joined the Army because, basically, I didn't want to go to school. The training I loved, the discipline I didn't. But since my army days, I have kept up with the training – I've bought my own gym!

LIFE OF CRIME

My first and only time in prison was because of drugs. But it was only a little bird, nothing much to talk about. I spent some time reading books. Believe it or not, I read yours!

DO YOU THINK PRISON IS A DETERRENT?

No. No way, because I walked into prison and it was like walking down the Old Kent Road, it was like being out on the street again. The only difference was there wasn't women there. Prison was great ... well, great-ish. The only thing I hated was missing the kids, because I wouldn't have them visit me. It's not right.

DO YOU BELIEVE IN CAPITAL PUNISHMENT?

Yes and no. The usual thing – for perverts, rapists, child molesters – yes. They're simply scum.

WHAT WOULD HAVE DETERRED YOU FROM A LIFE OF CRIME?

Having lots of money – that's the only thing, money. I was a bad boy at one point, a total arsehole. When I went to prison, I called my mother to tell her where I was and her answer was, 'Well, it took them 36 years to get you there but they got you there in the end.' She always thought I'd end up in prison and she was right. It doesn't matter who you are or how big or clever you think you are, the Old Bill will get you in the end. They always do.

HAVE YOU EVER BEEN STABBED/SHOT?

I've been stabbed once. And I've been shot at a couple of times but they missed – thank God! Both times I was working the door – once was in the club itself.

But when I was stabbed I didn't think, Oh, I won't do this any more – it didn't hurt. I didn't feel it at all when it happened. You don't feel it at the time – you feel it after. I think it's all to do with adrenalin. That red mist comes up and you don't see anything and you don't feel anything. You're in a fight – you just go for it. The red mist doesn't come up as much as it did – I'm more controlled now.

SCARIEST MOMENT?

It's hard to think of one. My scariest moment was working the door and I was tooled up. We bashed this geezer up and just tipped him down the stairs. The meat wagon's pulled up, the Old Bill's come running in. I've got a 3.57 Magnum stuffed down the back of my trousers. They came running in and said, 'You're nicked,' and I just said, 'Oh bollocks!'

Lucky for me, a friend saw what happened; she took the gun off me and slid out a back door. That was the worst moment of my life. I didn't want to go away for having a gun and not using it – that would be a mug off.

SADDEST MOMENT?

Missing my kids when I was in prison.

WHAT RATTLES YOUR CAGE?

Liars. I can't stand people who lie. I hate them.

HAVE YOU EVER REALLY LOVED ANYONE?

Yes. My kids. My wife. And my dogs. Not necessarily in that order – whichever way you want to take it. I have to watch what I say here!

WHAT FRIGHTENS YOU?

Losing my dogs. When I lost one of my British bulldogs it broke my heart. I had to have him put down because he was ill – then six weeks later the other one died. I was OK with the first one, but when it happened to the second one, too, it killed me, it really crucified me.

DESCRIBE A HARD BASTARD

A hard bastard isn't a bully-boy. I work on the door and I'm not a bully. I'm nice, I have style and I'm happy until they upset me and then I'll bash them. All these bully-boys around – they're not hard bastards. A hard man is a true man, I think.

NAME A HARD BASTARD

Phil Mitchell – only kidding!

I thought Lenny [McLean] was a hard bastard. I liked Lenny – I met him a few times and he was all right.

WHERE DO YOU SEE YOURSELF IN FIVE YEARS?

Hopefully rich, well off, comfortable – I'll probably still be on the door. Still be in the gyms. It's all a game but it's brilliant – it earns respect as well. You get a lot of respect, especially if you're on the right sort of door. Young blokes on the door are all so keen to bash everyone up, but really you don't need to be like that.

That's not my idea of things at all. My only reason to go to work is to earn some money, have a nice night and enjoy myself if at all possible. At the moment, I'm trying to break into something new – to do bodyguarding. I'm looking forward to that. To be honest, I don't have to work the doors any more, financially I mean. I tried giving it up but I was bored. To be truthful, I like the buzz.

I got into door work unintentionally, like most people do. The first place I worked was Bermondsey, just south of the river in London. I cracked me knuckles every weekend! It was rough. That was my first experience with a shooter – someone stuck a gun up my nostril!

These Bermondsey lads came down to the club and said, 'Let's shoot the doorman!' They came out with a .38. So I've got this gun to my head and the other doormen are at the top of the stairs and I thought, If they come down, I'm dead. For fuck's sake, don't come down those stairs. That was one occasion, another was I was standing in the Old Kent Road, when suddenly a red Ford Escort turns up and they shoot and I hit the ground very hard.

That's life on the door. You need to know who's who and what's what. I didn't when I first came to London. But I do now.

ANY REGRETS?

No. None at all. Whatever's happened has all been part
and parcel of life.

CONCLUSION

After the release of my last book, *Hard Bastards*, I came under a little bit of criticism because I didn't include Northern Hard Bastards, or Asian or Chinese, Liverpudlian or Scottish; the list went on ... So this time I have included them all. Yep, tough guys of all shapes and sizes, colours and creeds. There's a Hell's Angel – Marco probably came from one of the more difficult groups to interview. Kevin Chan – the kung fu supremo – intelligent, cool and calculated. Liverpool's own Charlie Seiga; The Iron Man of Bolton; Frenchman Kiane Sabet; Asian Kal – a mountain of a man – with the heart of a lion ...

All these men are from different walks of life; they are different in many ways but so alike in many others. A good percentage – in fact 40 per cent – of the men are not criminals, they are straight guys. Just because they are straight does not mean they're not tough. Many spoke of the 'red mist', an uncontrollable rush of adrenalin and anger so intense that it left them breathless with rage.

Whilst experiencing the 'red mist' most felt they were capable of almost anything. Seventy per cent of the men have, at one time, been stabbed. Each and every one agrees that, incredibly, they never felt the actual stabbing. But afterwards, in the cold light of day, it hurt like hell, especially when the knife was pulled out. Ouch! Ninety-five per cent of the men that had experienced prison agreed that it was a college where they learnt more inside than out. A better education and having money would be their biggest deterrent from a life of crime – not going to jail.

But what else did they have in common? Undoubtedly they all have an inbred sense of pride and honour. They would rather kill or be killed than let anyone take a liberty with them, that's for sure. Not one of the men I interviewed tried to make excuses for the things they had done, but neither did they apologise. Whilst researching for this book I met lots of 'retired' gangsters, villains, hoodlums and tough guys, all of them reformed characters. Nod, nod, wink, wink – know what I mean?

I'm not going to stand in judgement of these men. It was not my job to criticise them or challenge them on what they were telling me. That was not my intention. I knew just what they were capable of or I wouldn't have been interviewing them. I was questioning them as a journalist. I'm just reporting the facts like a war correspondent – yeah, that's it, a war correspondent. Because it is a war, and at times, whilst interviewing – or interrogating them as some of the men claimed I was doing – it felt like I was in the middle of a bleedin' war zone.

Cor, mate, these men can be paranoid and touchy. If any of them got wind of who I was interviewing for the book they would sneer, 'He's a tossa. What you talking to him for?' Or 'I'd do 'im any day.' It was like treading in a minefield. So I never mentioned who was in my book. I became sneaky, and lied. Yes, I admit it, I lied mercilessly and I don't care. It's my feckin' book and I put in who I feckin' well like! Oh dear, I just saw a bit of the red mist. I think I've been hanging around these tough guys too long ...

But, seriously, I didn't intend to get dragged into the politics of who's who and what's what. The only thing that mattered was this: is the geezer a tough guy? If the answer was yes, then I included them. If the answer was no, then I left him out. Plain and simple.

All the men in this book are as tough as nails. Hard core – they know the score!

I've heard it said that some of the men are tough on the outside and soft in the middle. Well, I suggest that you bite one and see ...

HARD BASTARD UPDATE

I'm often asked how the chaps from *Hard Bastards* are doing. Well, here's how!

ALBERT READING
At the tender age of 68, Albert has found love. He has a sweetheart. He also has a new job – minding a casino owner!

BIG JOHN
I was watching television the other night and was surprised to see Big John in an advert. In fact, he has been in several adverts. So things are looking good for him.

CHARLIE BRONSON
In June this year Charlie married the love of his life Saira in a quiet ceremony inside a top security prison. He is still serving life and is still kept in a cage. But both he and his wife are hopeful on a pending appeal.

CASS PENNANT
Life has changed for Cass. He is now a successful author and has written a bestselling book. He is currently working on a new book.

CORNISH MICK

I don't know what has happened to Mick, cos he won't tell me. Mick has been my friend for quite a number of years and he has and always will be a very private man. But I can safely say that he is alive and well and not in prison.

ERROL FRANCIS

Errol, his wife Sandra and his lovely family are happy and well. Earlier this year Errol made my day by asking me to be godmother to their son. I was honoured.

GLENN ROSS

The big guy has just won the title of Britain's Strongest Man for the third year running. In October he flys to Africa for the World's Strongest Man. 2001 is his year. Fingers crossed.

JOHNNY ADAIR

Johnny's life is a war. He is still fighting for his beliefs. Battling against the system and authority. He is currently back in prison in Northern Ireland.

BILL

Bill was arrested soon after *Hard Bastards* was released. He was tried and acquitted – of course!

RONNIE FIELD

Ron was sentenced to nine years in prison. He is due for release in October 2001.

JOHNNY FRANKHAM

They seek him here. They seek him there. They seek him bleedin' everywhere. Pssst ... somewhere off the M4.

FREDDIE FOREMAN

Gone fishing!

FRASIER TRANTER

Still hoping and wishing for word of his 'Fair Lady' – Martine McCutcheon. Please, Martine, put this big guy out of his misery.

FELIX NTUMAZAH

Not the sort of man I'd expect to hear much about. He just slips into the shadows and disappears.

STEVE ARNEIL

A straight, honourable man. The last time I spoke to Steve he was happy and well.

STILKS

Since the book and television show, Stilks is enjoying the success and fame and is writing his autobiography.

JOEY PYLE

Joe is currently in final negotiations with a major film company sorting out the film on Roy Shaw. But I can exclusively reveal that he has a new girlfriend. The old smoothy!

HARRY H

In recent months Harry has suffered a bout of insanity. At present he is ever so slightly unfuckinghinged. That aside, he is enjoying a full life as a recluse. Barking Mad!

ROY SHAW

Mr Shaw has become Mr Playboy since the release of his bestselling book *Pretty Boy*, the episode devoted to him in my TV show and the forthcoming film about his life. He has become irresistible to women. He is getting quite a reputation as a gigolo. One of his girlfriends was quoted as saying, 'Roy is as good a lover as he is a fighter!' WOW ... say no more!

BOBBY WREN

I haven't seen Bob or his gadgets for a few months. He may have seen me but I ain't seen him!

JOHN MCGINNIS

I saw Big John last week. He was happy and healthy and continuing to go about his business.

VIC DARK

Vic is happy with his girlfriend – Sammy. After his TV show, he has become a celebrity. He is currently in negotiations to write a book based on his life and time in prison.

THE BOWERS

The Peacock Gym is thriving and so are the brothers. Onwards and upwards. Go, Bowers, go!

KATE KRAY is the top ten bestselling author of Hard Bastards, a book which took the country by storm and was so successful it became a TV series for Channel 5, fronted by Kate herself.

Her marriage to Ronnie Kray gave her a unique insight into a world of criminal activity and has helped her to gain access to some of Britain's most notorious gangsters.

Kate's other bestsellers include Pretty Boy, the story of East End legend Roy Shaw and The Twins, Free at Last, the real story of Ronnie and Reggie. Killers, also by Kate will be published next year.

———————————

 GEOFF LANGAN was born in Dublin, Ireland. He has spent the last 20 years living and working as a photographer in England. Geoff has worked for publications ranging from Fetish Times to the Sunday Times. This is his first project with Kate Kray. He lives with his wife Rachel and son Patrick in South London.